Mud Running

Memories of Childhood
Inspired by a Fifty-mile Trail Race

By Richard E. Allen

Mud Running, Memories of Childhood Inspired by a Fifty-mile Trail Race. © 2011 Richard E. Allen. All rights reserved. ISBN 978-1-257-055142

Cover photo: On Table Top in the Uintah Mountains, 2009, Todd, Bryan, Chris, Dave, Dad, and Rich.

Contents

Preface……………………………………………….................. 1

Chapter 1: The Apprehensive Trail Runner……………… 5

Chapter 2: Bowser Todd, Man's Best Friend…………… 28

Chapter 3: My Big Sister Diana, and Snow……………… 45

Chapter 4: Cohleen: Sandcastles, Dirt Pies,
                           and Silly Mud…….. 63

Chapter 5: The Cottage Farm……………………………… 85

Chapter 6: Bunny Was Always There……………....… 101

Chapter 7: David, the Master Angler…………………… 123

Chapter 8: Chris the Musician……………………......… 149

Preface

My name is Richard E. Allen. The E stands for Elliot, which was a great source of embarrassment at Indian Hills Elementary. Many years before Pete's dragon shared the name, Elliot sounded far too distinguished and King's English for kids. Even my closest friends, Mike and Craig, thought it great fun to put on a Monty Python accent and call me by my full name.

"Richard," they said. "Richard Elliot, please come here," as if my mother were calling. "Richard Elliot, we shall go a-hunting today if the fog lifts from the moors."

Neither of my given names has any family history, and in fact, of four hundred years of ancestry that I've reviewed, the name Elliot never appears. My dad thought that it would look distinguished on an office door someday: Richard Elliot Allen, Master Architect. But I never became an architect, or an attorney like him.

I picture Don and Sandra Allen in the late 1970s. They've left their starter home and moved two miles up the east bench of Salt Lake City. Dad wears a three-piece suit in most every photo; even at birthday parties, he has the appearance that he just came from work. I imagined a demanding boss whose name was in as the firm's (Ray, Quinney, and Nebeker), disgruntled to let him go early. Especially, perhaps, for the birthday party of his fifth of seven children. *Overpopulating the earth*, the boss said. Dad kept his vest and tie on at home, as if the boss was still watching. Don B. Allen, Attorney at Law. Perhaps he intended for my name to be longer, more renowned, and to carry more weight with Mr. Ray or Mr. Quinney.

Mom wears the beehive hairdo and the green polka-dot dress of the era. She hides her fatigue well as Dad shines a blinding incandescent light at her so that the eight millimeter camera gets a good shot. Not too long with the expensive film, but just a quick clip to remember the day. Mom pretends to be delighted with the chimpanzee and trainer they've hired. A real live chimp in my basement to entertain a dozen boys at a birthday party. The birthday cake has ten trick candles on it—I'd blow them out, and they'd spark to life again. Decades later, my mom would ask us to clap the candles out to avoid spitting on the cake. But in the 1970s, we were free from such hygiene etiquette and reveled in homemade chocolate frosting, pink punch, and Life Savers candy.

"Richard the Lionheart," Dad said. "Great courage and strength." I'm embarrassed to confess that I didn't know who Richard the Lionheart was until this very moment, writing these thoughts, when I've researched it on my laptop. He was King of England almost one thousand years ago, fearless in battle and crusades. I don't feel that I've lived up to the name.

The memory of my childhood is something I've wanted to write for a long time. But it never quite came together. It takes more time to write a history than a busy adult is given. I hoped for a long plane ride without a movie, but I fall asleep too easily on planes. Perhaps a long rainy weekend with nothing to do but think and write. I haven't had one of those since 1993 when Heather was born, the first of my six daughters. Not until 2008 did an experience present itself, which allowed the spontaneous recollection of a thousand mind pictures: Squaw Peak.

This is the story of that fourteen-hour experience and the forty years of memories it evoked. But more than just a memoir, this is a tale of running. Squaw Peak was a day like no other in my life, a day of intense physical strain, mental anguish, and deep psychological reflection. An all-day trail race with no one to talk to gave me the opportunity to ponder the human qualities of those who shaped me and what I had become because of them.

Some feel that running is monotonous: the constant pounding on pavement, one foot after another, mile after mile. I disagree. Running is intense. It is ever changing. We run to feel the limit of what our bodies can do. We run to feel the lack of oxygen and energy, and then to regain it. Runners feel the texture of air, humid or dry, cold or hot, thick at sea level or thin on a high mountain. Beyond exercise, running is an acute encounter with the physical around us and inside us.

The varied experiences of running are symbolic to me. Each encounter is like meeting a person, interacting with that person, hearing his voice, shaking his hand, watching his body language. As we interact with that person over and over again, we become intimately acquainted. We know what's around the bend. We feel again what it's like to run past one mile, or three, or 26.2.

We want to interact again, to see familiar bright eyes, to hug and hold, to share a common funny story. Running is not easy, but we go back to it again and again. We want to shiver in the cold or sweat in the dry hot sun, to feel the difference between concrete and pavement or a trail layered soft with pine needles versus slick spring mud. Each day, each race, each person is different.

Associating running and memories was not in the plan. I did not sit down the night before and sketch out a root diagram of the recollections that would take me through the day. Some runners plan what they will think about from hour to hour to keep their mind occupied during a distance race. I was not one of them. And I was not reminded of childhood because of running, for I was a never a runner until my midthirties. Instead, sentimentality came unpredictably. It arose from odd things: a dog, a snowflake, a lonely road. Every trail took me back to the Uintah Mountains, the rocky overlooks reminded me of the H-rock road, the snowfall shivered out of me the memories of Solitude Ski Resort.

My childhood was privileged in many ways. I was neither poor nor rich, though some would accuse us of both. I recount years of grand experiences, from fancy vacations to tiny moments of play in the backyard. Most of all, I was blessed to know a large family. I interacted daily with eight different people, each unique, each intimately familiar with the character and flaws of the others. We went from contentious to loving; we were both supportive and neglectful, often irritated, and ultimately caring. I longed for the traits of my brothers, striving to be like them and to feel that they loved me. But it is the traits themselves that I recognize as the splendid diversity in life. As diverse as snow from rain, as warm moist sunshine from cold dry brightness, or as aspen from pine.

Recollections are sometimes painful. At times, they bore down on me during the run, like penance unrepaired. Regrets weighed on me exasperatingly, like an infidel desperate for the chance to return and retry.

At the same time, memories can give strength and perspective. Like a powerful tree, the roots of my past pushed me to soar upward with a leafy lightness unknown to my character. I felt the richness of life, the connection with the multitude of characters in my past that taught me about people and personality and individuality. Each of my six siblings was a figurative signpost along the road of youth, leading me, pointing the way, or simply being there for me to connect with.

I'll confess a couple of disclaimers. This story contains little or no mention of my parents. I sincerely honor my parents for their years of dedication and love, but I was told once by a college writing professor that parents and spouses are too close to write about. A story about family memories without including Mom and Dad may seem a great insult, as if they were missing from my youth. On the contrary, they were always there, for all of the memories. They deserve all the credit. Their influence and memory could fill several books. But writing directly about them is indeed difficult. Too emotionally close. Too nervous to offend or hurt those who've given all for me. Someday I hope to help them write their own personal histories, but in this book, their chapters are lacking.

On the subject of hurting and offending others, I have not asked permission to write about my siblings. I fear that some of my personal memories will displease my brothers and sisters. It's my hope that they will understand the subjectivity of personal memories. I'm not a perfect historian, and a few of the events I've described may be slightly different than factual. Conversations that I recall from thirty years ago are not flawless, and as with most nonfiction writing, the long-forgotten dialogue had to be embellished to fill in the storyline. And finally, I mean well. My intentions are good, and despite a few negative experiences in our history, you are still the familiar faces that I want to be with repeatedly. Like another run, as it were.

Chapter 1: The Apprehensive Trail Runner

Not since childhood had I felt the dual comfort and fear of sleeping in complete darkness in a cool damp basement bedroom. The comfort of being enveloped by darkness, wrapped in a tight cocoon where I would metamorphosize from fatigued sleep to rested wakefulness. But the fear of tiny sounds enhanced by blindness: a scratch above me, a creak in the other room, a drone just outside the window. Missing was the constant numbing hum of the fish tank air bubbles, my black Molly pets keeping watchful care of Bryan and me as kid brothers. I missed the bathroom bustle, just beyond my closed door, as my two teenaged brothers pushed the limits of bedtime with another hour of hubbub, a constant settling noise, and the reassurance that the two of us lying quietly in the dark were far from alone.

But here I was, alone, in an unfamiliar dark basement bedroom, wrapped in the sheets that smelled like someone else's mom had washed them. Despite my adulthood, thirty years removed from black Molly's attentive guard, I again felt the childhood fears of darkness. Not a monster under the bed or spiders coming down off the ceiling—though I won't forego that either of those also crossed my mind—but other anxieties that adults and children seem to share: Would I be okay, would someone be there for me, would anyone notice? The dark bedroom womb was the safer of two options, the other a venture out into a new and challenging life experience. An exciting experience—a trail race adventure, the culmination of almost a year of training, the ultimate outdoor challenge. But fearful experience nonetheless, and like a kid before the first day of first grade, I laid there with typical insomnia, basking in total apprehension of the dark unknown.

The mother whose detergent I knew was not my own, who had clearly raised a teenager or two in the basement bedroom now filled with food storage, was Terry Wolsey, married to my wife's cousin Brian. I would say "close cousin" despite twenty-five years in age difference, spread apart by generation and geography, and yet always known to me as a dear relative. Brian and I met when he was in the peak of his career as an obstetrician/gynecologist, and I was a fledgling college student who listed "pre-med" as a major and hoped to marry his cherished cousin Elizabeth. I wanted someday to be as successful a physician as he was, and as kind. But I was so many years away. "It's a long road," was the oft-quoted response to divulging my goal to be a doctor. It's as if you're never really an adult until you're a real doctor, often into your midthirties. And with Brian, I've never really felt that I got there, even after all the years of training, the MD behind my name, an extra year at Harvard for a masters degree, and several years of private practice. No matter how much you achieve, those ahead of you, like Brian, are still ahead of you. And worse, family medicine just doesn't hold the same clout as other specialties. I'm always a bit embarrassed by what I do, like the "waste products engineer" who doesn't want to admit that he's a garbage man, or a naturopath amongst a group of academics. I'm a family doctor, not a "specialist," but, as so often repeated to me, "just a general doctor, then."

The already tenuous situation with this wonderful cousin led to an awkward and procrastinated phone call, asking Terry if they had a spare bed I could use one Friday night in June.

"You mean this Friday night," she said. "You mean tomorrow night."

"Um, yes. Sorry for the late notice—if your house is packed with kids, I understand, and I can call someone else."

"No, no, it's fine," she replied. "Just the two of us and Angela nowadays—the brood's all grown and gone. We'd love to have you stay. What was it for?"

"I'm in a race," I tried to say boldly. "It's like a marathon, er ... well, it's an ultramarathon, which is like a double marathon. It's a trail race. And it starts up Provo Canyon, and I thought I'd save an hour in the morning by staying down there. I really don't want to be a bother."

"No, no, we'll be glad to have you. What time do you think you'll come?"

"Well, I'll probably come late if that's okay—like 10:00, and I'll get right to bed because I need to get up and leave by 4:00 AM."

"Wow—early race! I didn't think they started that early.

You know, I was in a 10k last summer …"

Terry continued her welcome to me and her description of a personal experience with running a race. I was relieved to have a place to sleep but continued that awkward feeling of not really wanting to admit what "race" I was about to do. She didn't seem to catch on that her distance and mine were almost ten-fold different, and the hour this sixty-year-old took to run the hardest race of her life would be just a fraction of what I was about to do. I did not feel mine to be superior, nor did I relish in the great exercise tolerance I'd developed and the strength I'd built up. I simply felt foolish. I hoped she would never catch on to the word "ultramarathon" and that I would leave her thinking that her race and mine were comparable.

A 10-kilometer run/walk is a reasonable, human-friendly distance. It's a great goal or accomplishment to follow a few months of increased exercise for the average person. It's approximately double what many people do every day on the stationary bike or treadmill as part of some sort of cardiovascular workout. A marathon, on the other hand, is a ridiculous biologically unsound distance with questionable historical authenticity and significance. There really isn't a 26.2-mile route to Athens, and if there were, the tradition or myth says that the warrior who ran it promptly died after his report. So why are we repeating the feat in modern day? Why do thousands of runners choose this as their ultimate objective, repeating it from year to year? And as if the famed Greek marathon isn't foolish enough, the ultramarathon adds shame to ridicule. Why would anyone run so long? What are you trying to prove? Some ultras are 100 miles and take sleepless runners through the night. Mine was just 50, seemingly easy in comparison to the longest but absurd when judged against a 10k.

The analysis of why we do hard things like marathons has beleaguered my life. I have too often asked myself why and not been entirely clear on the solution. Some would say that it's obvious, "showing off" like a little boy swinging on the monkey bars to make the first-grade girls notice him. But a marathon is not the best way to get attention from people. It can't simply be the desire for attention. Most anyone you tell nowadays has already done something similar and can one-up the tale with a race, or travel adventure, or award, or something. And the vast majority of us will never even come close to a rank among the winners of a distance race. We know that from the outset. From training, we already know approximately how long it will take to complete the race. We're not out to win or purely to show off.

  To "prove it to myself" is an oft-quoted rationale. Maybe so. Maybe running is a builder of self-assurance. The long months of training, increasing in strength and distance just a little bit each week. The added need to know not just that we can run three hours in the loneliness of predawn but that we can do it in broad daylight, in front of others, running with a bib number on the chest. Like a science experiment, we want to prove its repeatability. But after some repeat, why do we persist in seeking after another, and another?

  There is something intrinsic to running, some connection to our ancient ancestors, some purging in exhaustion. There is an elation, which is not happiness, for happiness is not found in vomiting and muscle cramps. It may be exhilarating but not in delight. It may be exciting but not with pleasure. We are like pilgrims who want to feel the weight of defiance but have no religious persecution to escape. We are Jews who won't deny the faith, even though no one is threatening our lives to do so. We want to feel what slaves and sufferers and martyrs have felt, but in our modern age, we have no natural cause to feel so. So we create a cause. It's a distance, or a mountain, or a seemingly insurmountable athletic feat. Maybe we do it because our lives are relatively easy, and we need the feeling of having it hard.

  My closest cousins lived in Provo, along with the familiar sight of beautiful square-topped Mount Timpanogas, the murky but shimmering Utah Lake, the big "Y" on the mountain, and the trapped smog that makes "happy valley" an oxymoron. Provo is home to the second-largest private college in the United States, Brigham Young University. The city had changed so much in the decades since I last visited Aunt Vivian that twice I took a wrong freeway exit and was late for a disappointing spaghetti dinner and prerace meeting.

  "There's more snow than usual," the thin, bearded man, our race organizer, announced to the pasta eaters. It was a crowded conference room at the Hampton Inn, the hotel where I later understood most runners were spending the night. "I want to thank Phil, who ran the entire trail last week and found about four miles of snow, including some tricky avalanche spots on the north side."

Some *oohs* and *aahs* filled the room, some a show of pride that the difficult race was now even more challenging, and a few like myself anxious with thoughts of sliding off the mountain. It was an eclectic bunch in that room, all very different yet bonded together with such similarity and all with the goal of finishing fifty miles on foot the next day. There were older runners, some approaching sixty, their rawhide skin and well-defined, thin facial muscles a sign of semiretirement in the brisk outdoors. There were skinny, skinny women, no more than a hundred pounds but all muscle, natural tan, ponytail, confident, and ready to run. There were middle-aged men, pale and balding, with farmer's tans and some thickness through the belly. These people, like me, fight to escape the office early or head out at 4:00 AM to fit some training time in between so many other demands. And a few young guns, early twenties maybe, boys who still wear their high school track T-shirts and could probably run the mountain twice without breaking a sweat.

"Phil also took the photos that you see on the Web site," the race director continued, his voice building up to something, "and he ran last week with a modern GPS unit, which has not only defined the fifty-mile trail but surprised us with something else." I expected fear and silence from the crowd but instead heard jeers and taunting, as if nothing—not even a secret hidden lake that we had to swim across—was going to stop these hardheaded and hard-bodied runners. The race director pointed to Phil as if to let him give the news, but then spilled it himself. "The actual elevation change is twelve thousand feet instead of ten thousand! I guess all those little ups and downs add another couple thousand feet to the big climbs."

I tried to act brave and unconcerned, smiling with the rest of the applauding crowd. But inside, I felt my heart wrench as the potential agony of this run was now exacerbated. The foolishness of my decision nine months earlier to set a goal for this trail run was pressing deeply into my temples, like an uncomfortable hat that neither fit me in size nor in style. My eyes felt the stress of a headache, not from sleeplessness but from anxiety, crowded in a room where I clearly did not belong. I don't know why the newly announced twelve-thousand-foot climb mattered to me. As if anything really made the difference for a novice—my longest run was thirty miles and five thousand feet of climb, so the difference between fifty miles or sixty miles or forty miles or twenty thousand feet of elevation change was all unknown to me. All potentially dangerous, and all extremely hard to consider.

The talk turned into irrelevant questions, or at least questions I didn't follow regarding certain sections of the trail and when our pictures would be online and where our families should park. The fellow next to me was equally bored, though without the unease that clearly marked my face. He looked familiar to me. Early thirties, Utah boyish looking but muscular and athletic.

"Hey," I held out a hand. "I'm Rich."

"Mark Scholl," he replied. "I was thinking you look familiar."

"Me too—college, I think. Weren't we in a fraternity together?"

"Not unless you're from Ohio," he said.

"Hmmm, maybe I've seen you in the office?"

"I'm an orthopedic surgeon at Salt Lake Regional," he replied with some dignity, as if the implication that he was seen in my office was an insult. If we'd met, it was obviously in his office.

"Oh, I'm at St. Mark's," I said, nodding my head as if it all made sense that doctors shared some common pathway that we all knew and recognized each other. I'd never been to Ohio, and we'd obviously not truly met before. Then, sheepishly, as a painful afterthought, I added, "Family medicine," and my usual defense of the underappreciated field, "I teach family medicine, actually. I'm on the faculty of a residency program there."

"Oh," he replied, disinterested. I almost thought that he didn't hear me. He looked away for a moment, as if something else caught his ear or in that way that people break eye contact when they didn't really hear or understand the last part of the conversation.

"Cold spaghetti." He turned back to me and started a new topic.

"Yeah," I laughed. "I should have gone back to the Spaghetti Factory instead." He looked toward the front of the room again. He didn't follow the word "back" and obviously didn't want to hear the explanation of my days at that restaurant. I didn't mean to impose the memory on him but just blurted out the first pasta comparison that came to mind.

Mark Scholl and I shared a few more comments, complaining about the sparse salad, the crowded room, and the unnecessary meeting. Complaints are something that strangers can easily share. Enthusiasm for the race ahead, or stories of training, would be shared by friends—or two who want to be friends.

Then suddenly, I pulled the ultimate doctor faux pas by asking an orthopod about my painful knee in a setting that was not his office. "It clicks a little," I went on, "not really painful but just a funny clicking—I think it's a plica or something." I tried to act knowledgeable, feeling abruptly aware of the usual condescending look that a specialist physician gives an inferior generalist. "Or maybe just a tendonitis …?" I trailed off in a slight question.

"Come see me in the office, and we'll see what we can do about it," he said. The "we" meant he and his office staff or his ortho buddies. At least, that's the way it always felt to me, like I was not a fellow physician or part of the upper circle of these chummy bone-cutting doctors. I'm sure he meant nothing of the sort, but my chronic insecurity makes me hear implications where there are none.

With that, I seemed to have ended the conversation, and I regretted it immediately. Mark wanted to get out of there, and now that I'd turned the talk to medicine, he didn't want to be burdened with diagnosing another complaining patient. It was time to focus on the run, to get a good rest, to clear his mind of people and work and talk and just concentrate on self and strength and the mountain. I felt the same, mostly, though my interest was temporarily sparked by the potential to visit with someone. Maybe share training stories—"share" meaning equally swapping stories with curiosity, not just me telling him things that he didn't care to hear.

I seemed to blow the chance for companionship. I seemed to be good at that. Something I said, or the way I said it, or just my demeanor. I'm not much of a fun-loving guy's guy that you want to hang out with. Never have been very good at that. I didn't feel that I fit well into my wife's family because of my self-absorbed, meek personality, a contrast to the slap-on-the-back man's man who communicates through sports anecdotes and uncouth jokes. Not that I'm a touchy-feely soft man who wants to hold hands and share feelings. I don't know what I am. I just know that I'd never belong in a Moose Lodge or such.

I got up and left just after Mark did, regretting that I'd ever come. I should have spent the evening at home with my family. I should have gone out to the Spaghetti Factory and relished in memories of my years as a waiter there. I should have relaxed with my kids and given them some of the time that I'd taken away in training the past few months. Relaxed with kids—as if that ever happened in my life. But maybe tonight would have been different. Maybe the enormity of the next day's endeavor would have humbled me into sharing sweet moments with my girls. I would have left the dishes undone, and not checked their rooms for clothes scattered on the floor, and not yelled at them for the Saturday work they'd not done the week before and would certainly do tomorrow. I would have just enjoyed being with them.

The hot June sun was starting its blinding descent over Utah Lake. I drove east to a shady parking lot near the university, turned off the car, and just sat for a moment. I wished for a view, either of the mountain or of the valley, but had neither. Like a sailor who wants to be at the bow and see where he's going or at the stern and see what he's leaving behind, but instead looks sideways to nothingness. I was alone again, with more time than I cared for to think about the race and what brought me to it. I sat for a long time without any answers, and then at dusk, I drove to Brian's house.

By 4:00 AM, I was in the car. I was riddled with anxiety over locking myself out of the house and forgetting something important I'd left—a shoe or a water bottle or something. Brian had demonstrated to me the night before how to turn the lock as I left and reassured me that I could knock if I needed to. But with all my heart, I didn't want to knock at 4:00 AM. I continued to feel such guilt for doing this crazy ultra, and I certainly didn't want to cause an early morning disturbance. *Leave no trace*, I thought as I closed the car door quietly. It was fairly cool for June, with a spit of tiny drops in the air.

The alimentary science of endurance athletics is at least as important as the cardiovascular training. I needed five thousand calories in the next twelve hours, but not too much at once, and a careful balance of long- and short-acting carbohydrates, proteins, and fats. Many a runner, my brother included, was ruined by the wrong mix, leading to stomachaches, cramping, vomiting, diarrhea, and potential total loss of energy. My car meal was carefully planned: a banana and two cups of orange juice as I left the house, dry Grape Nuts and Powerade as I drove up the canyon, and then a bagel just before the gun. No milk, nuts, granola bars, doughnuts, or yogurt. Both hydration bottles I would carry were filled with my home recipe of Powerade, heavy on the salt and light on sugar. My pack also held raisins, dry Oatmeal Squares cereal, fruit leather, and, for much later in the day, almonds. And unfortunately, in addition to careful planning for intake, elimination had to be given priority as well. I was hoping that my usual prerace apprehension and "runner's diarrhea" would kick in just before the race. Then I could spend the rest of the day just finding the occasional tree to pee.

My unfamiliarity with Provo haunted me once again. As I drove off into the dark quiet morning, I panicked about finding the right road and heading up the right canyon. I had mapped it out several times, knowing each road and exact distance. But still, I panicked. Anxiety was the story of the morning: what if? Forgetting something, taking a wrong turn, eating wrong, bowels not moving, stalling the car, wrong canyon, no place to park, no snow tires. Snow in June? No thought was left untouched as I drove along University Avenue. The deserted road lead easily to Provo Canyon, and as I started up the canyon, the little spit of rain turned into a little drizzle.

I parked in exactly the spot that I thought I would and laughed what little I could laugh at myself for the obsessive, neurotic way in which I had dreamed of and planned this day. The big day. One of the longest days of my life. A Saturday like no other. I drove up and angle parked on the side of the canyon road, about three cars in from the entrance to the park, just exactly the way I'd pictured it. Exactly as I'd seen it on Google Earth. Perhaps it was an omen that things would go just as I'd planned. Then again, I don't really believe in omens.

Vivian Park was abuzz with headlamps and flashlights. Early runners jogged in short stints, and then stretched out over picnic tables and playground equipment. Most wore slickers, as my mom called them, lightweight jackets that appeared slick from rain. As I organized drop-off bags in my trunk, I had a new thing to be fretful about: whether to wear a rain jacket or not. My experience was that perspiration inside the jacket was as bad or worse than allowing the rain to drench you from the outside. But cold was the real issue. If the rain continued all day, cold exposure would sap my strength like heavy November snow pulling down branches still burdened with leaves. I decided to wear a long-sleeve polyester shirt over my running shirt, two layers for warmth but breathable and lighter than my jacket. It was a plan to be soaking wet all day.

The drop bags, like everything else, were carefully calculated. A drop bag is something that the race volunteers take to an aid station, whichever number you indicate. A couple of those stations were accessible only by off-road vehicles, and one only by pack. Not wanting to saddle someone with unnecessary gear, we were asked to send little or nothing to number nine. But I knew I would welcome a change of socks and shoes at number six. Maltodextrin energy gels at the fifteen- and twenty-mile stations. Protein drink mix beginning at about twenty miles. Sunglasses and hat options at about sunrise, the second aid station. Each of my bags had a printed label, and I gathered them up and hurriedly went to drop them at the designated spot. The Web site indicated that drop bags not left by 4:30 AM might not get to where they were intended, a potentially dangerous mishap.

Runners are friendly folks, as I suppose any people who share a hobby are. If you collect guns, you'll enjoy visiting with others at the gun convention. *We're all in this together,* they seem to say, and even the competitive runner types gave a cheerful hello as they stretched out. I knew them from the attention drawn to them at the meeting the night before or from the way other runners spoke to them in deference and with slight bowing gestures, as if indicating monarchy.

Friendly with one another. *Then why do I feel so alone?* I thought. Like a vegetarian at a beef smorgasbord, I certainly felt out of place. As with the prerace dinner and orientation, I recognized no one there. I didn't see Mark. My brother mentioned someone he knew that would be running, but I would not have known his face or name.

The runners all looked so at-ease with their name-brand jackets, specialized hydration packs, and a familiarity as they talked about last year's event and other ultras they'd done.

"Never had rain before," I heard one say.

"Too hot last year, now too cold," another replied.

For me, it was all fumbling with unfamiliarity. I tried not to look daft as I searched for the right drop-bag location. I was still deciding whether to wear a headlamp or not and whether warming up was an additional few hundred yards of running I didn't need. I was surprised by a group gathered around the race organizer in the lighted pavilion, digging into several boxes of fresh doughnuts. Doughnuts were the last thing I wanted, and yet if these experienced ultra-runners were eating them, maybe I should, too. Was a glazed doughnut the ultra-marathoner's secret energy factor or just a common, easily provided treat for all groups and gatherings and almost certainly a gut-wrenching death wish within the first hour? Finally deciding against glazed rings and realizing there was not going to be an opening prayer, chant, or speech, I retreated to my car to wait out the half hour.

I have been a loner much of my life. Ironically, I can be a socially outgoing person. I like to lead a group. I like to teach a class. I left a lucrative medical practice to join a teaching program where I could oft be in front of student doctors. I still dream about the exhilaration I felt when I spoke at college graduation. But I'm sure when that speech was over, I walked home alone. I'm certain of it. I vaguely remember walking along Longwood Avenue with that post-success feeling of satiety but hungry for one-on-one companionship. I'm outgoing but not gregarious. I like to lead a group but not to be part of the group. Most runners train with partners and join in long runs once a week, usually Saturdays, with groups of four or five. I've never done that. Not once. In fact, I can remember only twice that I've ever run with a partner, both times with my brother Bryan. My hours were spent alone, occasionally wrapped up in headphones as if enjoying the company of a singer.

I even golf alone and enjoy it. I talk aloud to myself about how lousy my shots are, demeaning myself with shame. I don't mind being with others, but I also relish being alone. Relish and despise it, if you can feel both ways about something, like a good night's sleep for a person with a long list of things he wants to do. Without the sleep, he'll accomplish nothing, and yet a long slumber will steal time from his actions.

I like not having to fit anyone else's schedule. I'm on my own time. I'm surrounded by a big family and coworkers most of the day. The ten minutes twice a day, driving my black Volvo to and from work, I then enjoy the peaceful change of being all alone. I drive the car with purpose, and she demands nothing of me in return. There are no expectations of my behavior or actions. It's just me. Now at Vivian Park as I waited for the long day to begin, I sat in the familiar quiet Volvo womb, all alone.

My thoughts returned to Elizabeth and the uncomfortable conversation we had just a few hours before. I sat up in bed and checked my e-mail one last time, the blue light from my laptop illuminating the tiny basement room. It was crowded with food storage, ancient exercise equipment, and an abandoned turntable stereo system. An antique hope chest was at the foot of the bed, and I was reminded that I promised Elizabeth one for our tenth anniversary. That was six years ago. A small refrigerator buzzed in the adjacent room. I decided to make the call.

"Heather showed me the Web site of your race," she said. "You didn't tell me how long it was."

"I said that it would take me all day," I replied innocently.

"You said that it was a trail marathon." She was on the verge of tears or anger, and the combination was the worst possibility.

"I just didn't think it really mattered," I said. "It's a trail race that will take me all day."

"*Fifty* miles! That's insane. That's just not safe."

"I'll be fine, hon."

"I just feel like you lied to me about this race."

"I didn't lie …"

"You purposefully avoided telling me how long it was."

I was silent, caught with guile. From the moment I started running, it was uncomfortable for her. That time when I came home with my arms raised in victory, having finally broken the one-mile mark that had escaped me since teen years. The marathon books from the library, which she'd found in my car, like a kid caught with porn magazines. Running meant less time with the family. It was a change in our life plan. It didn't fit in with the marriage we'd started and lived. It was something new and different. An early "midlife crisis." Next thing, I'd be driving a little red convertible.

"Anyway," she said, "I want you to be safe."

"Thank you for your concern."

"And have fun," she said. "I'm not sure whether to be angry or to wish you well."

"I understand," I said. "I'm sorry that you feel that I lied to you." I chose my words carefully, as usual. Admitting fault is not my forte. I hate to feel guilty, even when I am. Ever since I was eleven and Mrs. Call caught me dumping out desk cleaner so I could use the bottle for a squirt gun, I didn't like feeling guilty. I was the master of innocence, saying whatever needed to be said to explain a misjudged situation.

Guilt is a virtue I can't seem to shake. Moving the whole family to Boston on a sort of whim. Leaving Elizabeth's Canadian hometown and moving back to Utah. Losing interest in gardening and fruit trees and instead pursuing money and position at work. "It's all for the family," I explained, as most fathers who spend very little time kicking a soccer ball or helping with science projects.

"I'll see you at the end, then," she said after a long pause.

"Yeah, if it works out—I don't want to be a bother."

"You're not a bother—you're my husband!" The anger rose again.

"I just mean ... I mean ..." I drew in a breath. "I mean thank you for being there, and I'll be excited to see you."

"I love you," she said with a rising tone of reminder, like she does after she yells at the kids right up to the doorway, and then wishes them well as they step off to school.

"I love you, too." My tone was more exasperated, quiet, apologetic; I wished the situation were somehow different, that I didn't feel guilty.

I hung up the phone and closed the laptop. My eyes were dry and tired, though I'd been unable to sleep. My plan for seven hours of sleep had now dwindled to four. The thought of backing out briefly crossed my mind. But then I must have fallen asleep.

Now I sat in the car in a silent drizzle, chewing on a dry bagel, and the race was about to begin. Recalling that conversation troubled me again: Why was it that I couldn't fully disclose to her the details of this race? Six months prior, we sat at the Training Table restaurant together, where she confessed to me that she had a huge goal in mind: reacquiring her registered nurse license. It would take intense study in the coming months, and for me, that meant Saturdays with the kids while she went to the library. She was tearful as she expressed her desire to accomplish this thing, and I was fully supportive. I in turn confessed my own goal: to run the Salt Lake Marathon in April.

I believe that's the point where I also mentioned the "trail marathon" in June, without admitting that this fifty-mile climb was my real goal. I couldn't understand my inability to tell all that to her, especially at a time of close confessions. Through months of winter training, I still never entirely confessed. Like a boy secretly saving to buy his mother a Christmas present, I couldn't reveal my preparation and possibly hoped something would interfere—the race cancelled or my leg broken. Hers was an honorable goal, to renew the license that she'd worked so hard for in college. Mine seemed frivolous in comparison, a meaningless leisure pursuit that earned no money, diverted me from family time, and caused me to be self-engrossed for ten hours per week.

The group of doughnut eaters was dispersing from the pavilion and headed toward the start line. Headlamps bobbled and turned, like a school of neon fish headed into a dark cave deep beneath the ocean surface. I exited the car to join them. I paused to consider the jacket once again, decided against it once again, tightened the water bottles on my belt, and felt ready to do this race. I joined the school of fish, all in good spirits as they joked about who should be at the front of the group.

I noticed that everyone had their number bibs folded small and pinned to their shorts. I was the novice here, with my bib pinned to the back of my shirt. I awkwardly reached around and started to unpin the bib and was still working with pins and twisted clothing when a "Three … two … one" countdown startled me, and the runners started to run. There was no gun and no fanfare. This was the simple start to the big race, and I was still fidgeting with my bib number and lost a pin on the dark asphalt as the runners—all of them—ran past me. It was probably less than a minute, but the start area was empty when I finally got my bib folded and pinned to my shorts. Loner once again. Sort of symbolic that my big day started this way, like an omen that I was not meant to be there. The group was several hundred yards down the dark mountain path when I finally crossed the unpainted start line and started to jog.

I felt really, really good. Except for poor sleep and the bib mishap, things had gone well, and I felt energetic. Within just a few minutes, I was part of the group as we passed by Bridal Veil Falls, the stunningly beautiful waterfalls heard but unseen at 5:00 AM in the darkness and fog. We were on a downhill path, and I easily passed runners until I was almost at the front. I was trying to hold back and go easy, recalling my April marathon experience of fifteen strong, fast miles followed by eleven of fatigue and slowness. But it was downhill, and I was excited, and all the worries and cares that discomfited me were a mile back, left behind with the jacket and the car and one lost safety pin at the start line.

I cannot say that I've ever been heroically successful as an athlete. I played basketball pretty well until age thirteen or fourteen, when all my friends grew taller and I did not. I always dreamed of dunking it—a feat at five feet six inches, but I was determined. Determined to spring into the air like Michael Jordan. But the determination and the goal to dunk only lasted a week or so, and then I was back to reality. My friends only called me to play ball when they were desperate for a fifth man.

I was a good defensive soccer player, earning the nickname "Animal" because of my aggressive style, a few illegal tackles, and a few yellow cards. But soccer didn't take me anywhere. Despite having three of the state's top players, our team suffered from transient coaching, a lack of unity, and by midseason a total loss of confidence.

Baseball was clearly my worst sport. I earned the "Strikeout King" award in my final year: eighteen strikeouts, more than any player in the league. With six innings per game, I had enough strikeouts that I'd lost one entire game for the Utes. I played center field, where there was rarely any action. I did hit a home run once: a hard swing with my eyes closed. Coach Mel was more shocked than I was.

Mostly, I was a walker. In the years after college, when I realized that a twenty-something-year-old body needed exercise, I turned to walking. I would sometimes carry five-pound hand weights or throw in some push-ups or sit-ups as part of a workout—but mostly just walking to enjoy the morning air, to meditate and pray, to enjoy the scenery, and to help keep my body in some sort of physical shape. I can walk a long way and can hike like the "Mountain Goat" nickname my brothers gave me on King's Peak. But I never thought I would be a runner.

I am not sure what hit me in October 2002 that I should become a runner. It was just days after Brynn's birth, and perhaps I was restless to get out. I was enticed by the challenge, having finished many years of schooling and now left dry of academic achievements. There were no more A's to get or tests to take, and my career was on a plateau without hint of future ascent. I needed a new challenge and became set on trying to overcome a longstanding fear of distance running. I had a strong mental block beyond a half mile, not to mention the real physical strain that my body didn't manage well in running. Golf season was over, and the first snow had covered the Canadian plains, and something inside me wanted to run.

Suddenly, I had library books on my desk on how to train for a marathon, and I found myself searching the Internet for spring and summer events. After all, runners don't just settle for 5k and 10k. The marathon is the must-do achievement, and Mom said I was an achievement-oriented person. I dove into this idea that I would become a runner. Yet despite my enthusiasm, I silently wondered, *Can I really pursue something so large, so lofty? Or will it be yet another short-term false-hearted attempt, like dunking a basketball?*

Besides soccer practice, the last time I ran was age ten. It was my friend Dallin's idea, the morning after we watched *Rocky* at the Tower Theater. We couldn't quite find the courage to swallow raw eggs like Rocky did, but we were up early in the beautiful June sunshine and determined to run and train hard. Unfortunately, we only made if halfway around the block, and then cut through Rod Snow's backyard to come home for a Super Sugar Puffs breakfast. That was it. Running was hard.

October 22, 2002, 8:35 AM, was cool but sunny as I headed out to the end of my gravel driveway. The small town started bustling a little bit this time of morning, the kids having just been dropped off at school. No passersby would know that I was about to face one of my life's greatest challenges. Like an invalid about to walk, it would be no less than a miracle if my legs would take me a mile. I had carefully measured distances around the neighborhood in my Volkswagen Jetta a few nights before.

I started a slow jog. It felt good and easy, and for at least three hundred meters, I felt like I would accomplish my goal. I was surprised at the ease at which it came, like gliding down a river with a little effort only to steer and keep the canoe straight. I must have been smiling, though I rarely do. Then, as usual, I felt the strain at a half mile. My legs ached, my chest burned from sucking in dry air too hard and too deep, and my diaphragm muscle started to pinch. I remembered running to Scouts from my house, a Tuesday night, almost dark, age twelve. My diaphragm pinched, and I grabbed it beneath the Scout badges on my shirt and wondered if I was having a heart attack. The pain stopped instantly when I stopped running and instead walked. If the pain stops, it must be that man is not meant to run. I must stop running. I always stop running. Half mile is the point where I stop. I'm a quitter. I'm the Strikeout King. I can't dunk the basketball. I never catch fish.

This was the moment, so trivial and insignificant and yet so immense. What separates mediocre from great. Beyond the point where it burns. Somehow I had the mental capacity that morning to not stop. I decided to go on this time, even if just this one time. What if I continued on and on—would I pass out? Would I permanently damage my legs? Would I give out and fall on the pavement, attracting the attention of neighbors and getting rushed by ambulance to the very hospital where I worked?

I pushed and pushed, feeling more of the dryness and burning in my chest. I remembered running in Monterey, past the Pebble Beach golf course, paired with my brother Bryan. I must have been fourteen. We weren't runners, but we went for a jog because it was easy. The air was moist and felt good going in and out of my throat. The altitude was sea level, and coming from our Utah elevation, it felt like an infusion of oxygen, like steroids pumping up our muscles. We felt like strong California boys and had the unrealistic hope that our long run on vacation would be the equivalent of running at home. It was not.

There was a short incline that I thought would never end, though it was only about two hundred feet. Up and over, and then a slight downhill and on to flat ground. I was certain that my loud and rapid breathing could be heard all around. My mind pushed my body on, determined to overcome the one-mile obstacle that had been mentally blocking me for twenty years. And finally, I did it. 1.2 miles. The full distance, plus a little more, just in case I measured wrong. It was no small event in my life.

Anxious to see if I could repeat the effort and surprised at how little my legs ached later that day, I was up and going the very next morning. This time, it was 1.5 miles, cruising past Ray Viola's house like the veteran runner that he was. I knew that once I had broken the one-mile mental block, I could push my body more and more and know that I was not going to die in distance running. I came home covered in sweat, walking through the front door, raising my arms in great triumph. Elizabeth looked at me unhappily, wary of this new thing. I'm surprised she didn't cry at that moment. I was already facing a crisis at work, and we had a new baby, and an extra hobby was not what we needed.

I kept a journal of my daily runs. *October 30, 2002: 1.9 miles, −5 degrees F, frigid, clear, and dark. Felt very good, and not as hard to complete the last leg. Oreo the dog does well off a leash at this time of morning.* Within two weeks, I was doing about two miles every weekday. Once I even included the south hill, a steep one-third-mile climb that forced me to walk halfway. On my birthday, November 11, I finally did the elusive nonstop five-kilometer run.

Soon, I was finding new routes and places. The cemetery road was particularly difficult, as I always hit a strong wind out to the west. Running through town was nice in the very early morning, but by 7:00, there was too much traffic, even for a small town. Through the school playground, out by the golf course, and then along the river and back became my favorite route, exactly 5k. Before Christmas, I knew I had to try a longer run and incorporate increasing long runs in my weekly routine. *Dec. 16: Trying to be like Rocky at 6:00 AM, but my hip is bothering me again. I ran to the cemetery and did okay. Felt well enough to do another 5k. I was surprised at how loose and good I was feeling between 8 and 10k, running slowly but breathing easy and feeling fine.*

A break at Christmas brought my hip tendonitis under control, and I continued my running at 5k a day and doubled that once a week. I am not a fast runner, coming in at 24 minutes for my fastest 5k. I ran 12k in just over an hour on Valentine's Day. Then I started adding some 400-meter sprints and hill climbing to the routine, based on articles in *Runners World* magazine. March 3: *New snow and very chilly. A nice morning run.*

My brother Bryan says that we're genetically plagued by a low VO_2 max—the total amount of oxygen consumption that a body can handle per minute. Mine improved some with training but was essentially a genetic gift, or lack thereof. This and the continuing stiff tendonitis in my left hip made me ease up a bit. A trip to Hawaii drained me completely: almost two weeks without running, plus jet lag and laziness. I had a hard time building up again. Busier than ever, and readying to move to Boston that summer, I knew that training for the July 24 Deseret News Utah Marathon was not an appropriate priority. My new hobby would have to wait a while.

I searched for some other culminating event for my training. After a successful eight-mile trial run on April 1, I came home and sent in my application for the April 12 University of Lethbridge race, all ten miles of it.

The intimidation was profound, and I started to feel what high school dropouts must feel in talking with graduate-level professionals. We may all be human, and similar, but our education and experience makes us speak a very different language. In the prior few months, I had been seen running by just enough eyes that I was now known as a runner. Little did they know that I'd actually never run in a race and that I couldn't run more than a mile until October of last year. But suddenly, I was buddying up with Greg Burt, the fifty-year-old town administrator who ran St. George in just over three hours last year, and Ray Viola, who was disappointed with his Deseret News time of two hours, fifty minutes. Ray's the kind of guy who probably runs a five-mile "warm-up" early in the morning before the ten-mile race starts.

I received a call from the town newspaper. "This is the *Star* calling to ask about your entry in the U of L race. How are you feeling right now?" I just told them that I hoped to finish, and a 1:40 time would surprise me.

I did all the right things: the pasta dinner night before, up early for a light carbohydrate breakfast, mentally preparing myself for the challenge as I drove to Lethbridge. But still, there are little details that a first-timer doesn't know: How do you put your race number on? (Safety pins.) How do I get my clothes to the other end and get back to my car? (Shuttle.) How do you know where the course is if you've never run it? (Follow the signs.) Do they serve Gatorade or just water? (Both.) I was glad to have Greg and a couple of his friends there to talk for a while and get the race jitters out of me. Then, the time came.

"Well, shall we go line up?" Greg asked. I was terrified as I followed these experts to the front of the line.

After a chilly few minutes waiting for the start, I heard a countdown and a shot and boom—we were off. Suddenly, everyone around me was moving fast, and I felt like I was in Spain, and the bulls were behind us, and I was about to get trampled. *Pace yourself.* I remembered the simple advice from every person I ever talked to about racing. I tried to slow down, but my usual eight-minute-mile pace seemed to carry me ahead of the pack. *Maybe I'm better at this than I thought,* I considered in the early eagerness of my first race.

Running along Scenic Drive was great. I felt very good—good pace, good breathing, comfortable terrain. I had promised myself that I would stop and walk for one minute every two miles, as one of the books advised novice runners. But no way was I going to stop now, not while everyone else was cruising on past me.

I checked in the three-mile mark at twenty-four minutes, exactly as expected. I kept going strong for about five miles, and then purposefully walked for exactly one minute. We were down in the valley along the river, and I was feeling the strain and glad to walk.

Nothing prepared me well for the hill of death. That hill still goes through my head. I see myself on the hill, runners ahead, struggling to pump up, some walking. I was falling behind. I wanted to push harder, but the strain was greater than I'd ever experienced in all my days of hiking and soccer and running. And there was no end in sight. A full one-mile steep hill. The image would stay with me for months to come and put a temporary end to my quest for races. Any thoughts of a future marathon vanished from my mind. That one-mile hill was so hard. When I finally reached the top, I was able to jog again, but in a daze and very slowly along the bluff.

Elizabeth and the kids were just getting out of the car as I came along the final two hundred yards. Instead of cheering and waving, the kids just stared at me going by, as if they didn't recognize me. Running was as new to them as to me. What was Dad doing? I finished in 1:22, just about my expected time. I was so glad to be done and to walk around for a few minutes. I tried to snack on bagels and bananas, but my tummy was upset and would be the rest of the weekend.

For a week, I ached all over and wanted nothing but rest all the time. It should have been enough to drive me from running ever again. But it's hard to forget those months of training: three hundred miles on my Saucony shoes, gallons and gallons of my own hydration recipe, cold quiet mornings of exercise, and the race day excitement of my first-ever event. It all swirled through my head for months afterward, even the hill of death. *Perhaps if I worked on my hill training a little more,* I thought. What if I just pushed a little harder? A few more years, and I would be out of the thirty- to thirty-nine age category. Maybe then I could consider training for the 26.2 miles. Perhaps living in Boston, home to the world's most well-known marathon, I would be inspired. Then maybe, just maybe, when I returned, closer to age forty, ready to run again, I could reach that great runners' goal.

Boston came and went in a quick year. I ran very little there, maybe 5k a couple of times per week. After that, another year passed in Canada, with the busyness of life precluding a successful running career. It wasn't until I moved to Salt Lake City that I was reinspired to really run again. Living less than a mile from Millcreek Canyon was the major impetus. Now running wasn't just exercise and training for an event but an escape to the mountains. Just like when I was a kid and could climb the trails above my house or follow the gulley down through the golf course or drive to the Uintas. Every day, I could spend a few moments in true wilderness.

I trained slowly, enjoying the canyon as much or more than preparing myself for a race. A 10k my first year. A half marathon two years later. Finally an attempt at the Salt Lake

Marathon in April 2008. My first-ever marathon did not go well, and I was tempted to quit running altogether. But reviewing my training, it occurred to me that a road marathon was not going to be my strength. I enjoyed climbing more than descending. I loved the cold outdoor mornings with challenges of sleet and wind. I wanted to be in the mountains and hike all the time, not just pound my feet on pavement. Running was an attempt to substitute for hiking. It was something I could do every day, where hiking can only be done half the year and in good weather and with more time. Trail running was my real desire.

On a sunny but cool afternoon in late September 2007, I left work at 2:00 and drove to Little Cottonwood Canyon. It was my "administrative" time at work, two half days per week that I spend doing research and paperwork. I felt guilty leaving the office and sneaked out the back door, still wearing my tie. Then, in the dark of the parking garage in the backseat of my car, I stripped down and donned my running clothes and shoes. I drove to the White Pine Lake trailhead and knew I had been there before but not for decades. There were no other cars in the parking lot, no one hiking on this weekday afternoon. A few days later, everything would be blanketed with snow, and the canyon would be given up to skiers until May or June. But I caught it just in time for a beautiful fall run.

I had a new iPod Shuffle that I got free when I renewed my credit card. I'd never run with music before, cumbered by a CD player that jostled off my hip when I tried and wanting to be out in nature and hear the nothingness without interference of artificial sounds. But convinced by my brother that music can liven up a run and armed with the tiny iPod, I plugged in the headphones, and then stashed my car keys under a tire. I laced up my shoes, and then turned and stared up the giant granite mountain. Then I started to run.

I played the same song over and over again, "Keep Holding On" by Avril Lavigne. It was a pop song that I'd heard on the radio and reminded me of its associated movie *Eragon*. The movie fit my feeling: flying like a dragon high above the rocky cliffs in Europe. I ascended quickly and could see my tiny car below and the distant city just coming in to view. The rocks on the narrowing trail grew larger as I climbed: tiny gravel turning to fist-sized rocks, and then bread-loaf stones, and near the top car-sized boulders in a massive rockfall below the summit. The rocks were like raised platforms holding me high above the thick and heavy earth. I felt as light as the cool thin air, the sunshine, and the mild breeze. My Asics gel shoes bounced me from one step to another, my chest alive with breath as I expanded for air more than ever before. Near the lake, I launched from one boulder to another, hopping quickly toward my goal with energy that came from autumn magic. Just me and the pika, the tiny mammal I could hear squeaking as I intruded on its high-mountain home. A diminutive figure, like that in a Chinese painting, hopping from granite boulder to boulder, alone in the gigantic alpine cirque.

Finally, I made the lake. Three miles, over a two-thousand-foot climb, in an hour and sixteen minutes. I almost jumped in the lake, I felt so high. I could feel the sweat glowing in the bright sunlight and wondered how I would explain my sunburn at work the next day. I guzzled from my water bottle, walking around the lake on the rocks, staying above the muddy shore. It was not my longest run, nor my highest hike. But it was a combination I'd never appreciated before: running up a mountain. Trail running. It felt marvelous. It was at that moment, standing at White Pine Lake, gazing at the towering mountains around me, that I became a trail runner. It was the beginning of the greatest event of my life.

Chapter 2: Bowser Todd, Man's Best Friend

At the Squaw Peak fifty-miler, our time on smooth pavement was brief. After passing Bridal Veil Falls, we came upon a glow stick and a shadowy human figure pointing to a dirt trail, which commenced the mountain climb. The paved trail was wide enough to pass each other, but the new trail was a single track. The sudden stop to wait my turn was startling, but at least I was only following a dozen or so runners and not the full two hundred. We started up a trail I'd never seen before, and yet it was as familiar to me as all the Wasatch mountain trails I've been on these many years: the same scrub oak and grasses and brown clay-like dirt. The runners were close together, each tailgating so as to push a fast pace from behind. I was glad that the holdup was minimal, and we were moving on with this race. I was not so much anxious to finish and get it over with but eager to get beyond what I'd run before. To see what it felt like. To see if I could endure. And perhaps I was restless to be alone again, in my comfort zone of running without a group.

It was then I faced one of the most significant problems of the day: I was following a dog. It seems ridiculous, but it was unexpected and troubling for me. I hate dogs. It was a yellow lab or retriever—one of those big dogs that everyone loves. It was unleashed and followed closely behind a short, fit woman with a blonde ponytail. I wondered whether she intended the dog to run the full fifty miles or just start the first couple of hours with us. Most of all, I wondered how to get out of the situation. I do not like dogs.

My dislike for dogs must have begun with Rusty, the Irish Setter who readily tackled me at a meager six years old. That's all I remember of Rusty—that he climbed and tackled and slobbered a lot. I watched my oldest sister pull porcupine quills from Rusty's underbelly once, a task she took on because my parents were gone, and no one else dared. She used huge vice grip pliers as Chris held tight to the yelping dog. Rusty didn't stick around much longer. The police and the zookeeper were at our house one day, discussing Rusty's tendency to jump fences and go chase sheep at the zoo. I was mortified by the thought of an animal being put down, yet I was secretly glad to be rid of Rusty and to feel that our house was no longer overrun by a big wagging tail and dirty long red hair.

A few animals came and went after that. A little stray dog underfoot, unnamed in my recollection and gone as quickly as he came. Patches the calico cat, a mean, scratchy, shifty creature whose run-over corpse I discovered one day on my way to fifth grade. Again, the shock was great, but the mourning was brief. Fish, hamsters, frogs. Nothing long-lasting, human friendly, or unforgettable.

But the six kids always wanted a dog, and I, being a kid of impressionable age, also begged for a canine companion. I had yet to recognize how much I disliked Rusty and his kind. Chris, at fourteen, was most adamant about a dog: a teenage Frisbee companion necessity. Dave was twelve and insisted he would care for its every need. A big family needs a dog. A family with three-quarters of an acre of yard needs a dog. Our annual family Christmas photo was missing that one thing, a dog.

There would be no dog, my parents announced. My dad despised animals as much as I now do. The grimace on his face as he dealt with the big uncontrollable dog was unforgettable. Mom, on the other hand, sympathized with the kids' need for animal companionship. She talked of a little indoor dog, but Dad wouldn't hear of it. Perhaps a medium-sized garage dog. Dad held firm. Finally, in 1976, it was announced that there would be no dog at all. Instead, there would be a baby. A seventh child, Spencer Todd Allen.

Mom was in her forties already, and the health risks of pregnancy weren't lost on me, even at age eight. Diana was sixteen, ambivalent about a cute little baby that she was old enough to mother, while at the same time hesitant to add to an already crowded household—and old enough to be aware that others would criticize our overpopulating the earth.

My brothers wasted no time giving this new baby a dog nickname. As with many family names, it would stick for decades to come. Even thirty-year-old Dr. Spencer Allen, DDS, is still affectionately known to family, friends, and coworkers by the name we unofficially christened him out of resentment for lack of a dog: Bowser.

Bowser: "plays well with others." Nothing could be more true of our youngest brother. "Man's best friend." He was heavily mauled as an infant. Everyone wanted to hold him. Everyone wanted to be seen in home movies with the new baby. He was the pet we'd waited so long for. He was all the fun of Rusty, Patches, and Bilbo the teddy-bear hamster, but he didn't leap on you, scratch at you, or gnaw your fingers. Bowser was a hit from Day One.

If there is a natural division in our family, it is between fourth and fifth, Bryan and me. Bryan was like the youngest of the older four, and I the oldest of the last three. They remember lots of camping trips, the Wasatch Drive house, and roast beef gravy with tomato soup poured over rice as Monday night leftovers. We remember plane trips, Hawaii, Washington, DC, and New York. We moved to the Canterbury Drive house when Bowser was just a year old. He grew up on roast salmon and fresh imported string beans, things my parents could only afford in their later years. Some would say Bowser was spoiled as a youngest child. I would say he was well loved.

He was only six when we flew to Washington, DC, for a family vacation. "Family" being the last three kids with Mom; Dad would join us later. It was my first plane ride, but one of dozens that Bowser would enjoy in his childhood. None of us would ever quite recover from that injustice. And it wasn't just one plane ride but a series of five or six. "The milk route," Mom called it. The cheapest way Continental Airlines could get us back east.

We flew from Salt Lake City to Houston. Todd, as he was known when Bowser didn't seem right, was remarkably fearless. He was invited by a cute young stewardess to see the cockpit and meet the captain. He returned to his seat, beaming with pride and posing with plastic wings pinned to his chest. I was old enough to worry when the plane rumbled into the sky, and loud hydraulic noises brought the wheels up. But Todd loved it all: peanuts, pop, little pillows, little potties.

"Do we stay on this airplane from Houston to Haustin?" he asked Mom. To this day, we tease him about "Haustin, Texas." We did fly to Austin, and then to Memphis, and finally to Baltimore. A full day of airport bookshops, toting luggage, and lunching on peanut butter sandwiches on heavy homemade whole wheat bread.

Our first series of plane rides was followed by our first cab ride. It was dark, and the seasoned traveler, Dad, wasn't with us; we were confused as to why we flew into Baltimore when we were supposed to go to DC. Mom had thirty-five dollars cash and detailed instructions on where to hail a cab, what to tell him, how much to pay.

"Key Bridge Marriott," she told the cabbie. "I am told it will be a thirty-five-dollar trip."

"Yes, ma'am," he said with my first hint of an eastern accent, "about a forty-minute trip." She uncomfortably sat in front while the three of us belted up in the backseat of the cruiser. I had never seen my mother in such an awkward position or heard her make conversation with another man. Later in life, I would discover that her social skills were unmatched, when a thirty-minute electrician visit ran over two hours, with the man opening up and tearful about his family and his life. But on a dark night, in a place that was not home, Mom and the kids were reserved and nervous.

Nervous kids—except Todd, that is. It was all fun for him. I was just old enough to recognize the tension of the situation. What if he dropped us off in these dark woods somewhere? Maybe he wasn't taking us to DC at all, but an alley or warehouse in Baltimore. Maybe he had a gun. Todd, at six, saw and felt none of that apprehension. He loved the plane taking off and landing. The big airport. The way your luggage came out on a moving conveyor, a "chugger," as he called it. Then a friendly, haggard-appearing cabbie with an accent.

"Had a fella wanted to go to Chicago once," he said. "Hopped in the car and asked, 'How long is your shift?' 'Beg pardon, sir?' I said. 'I need to get to Chicago, and there're no more flights,' he said. Now, Chicago's a long way, sonny. D'ya know how far Chicago is?"

He looked at Todd, who smiled and looked up at me.

"It's a long ways from here," the cabbie said. "Ya see, we're on the coast—on the ocean—and Chicago is on the Great Lakes, almost in the middle of the country. Where you from, son?"

My terror peaked. A stranger was asking us where we

were from. It was the classic scenario. He may as well have asked, "Do you want some candy?" and then asked if we'd jump in his big dark van to go home with him. *Your mommy wants you to come with me ...*

"Where'd you come from today, son?" He looked straight back at Todd in the rearview mirror. I tried to motion with my enlarging eyes that he should not answer.

"The west," I blurted out. But it was too late.

"Utah," Todd said with a big grin. I grabbed his arm and signaled for him to be quiet.

"It's okay," Mom said, turning around from the front seat and seeing my concern.

"Utah?" the cabbie repeated. "Utah, now there's a place I haven't been. Wonder how long it would take to drive to Utah."

"How long did it take you to Chicago?" Todd asked self-assuredly.

"Drove all night," the man said. "Drove all night and then some, 'bout twelve hours, with him sleepin' in the backseat there."

"That must have cost a fortune," Mom joined in, more relaxed and friendly now.

"Near five hundred dollars," he said. "Problem was, when I got to Chicago, I had to turn around and come home. Nobody paid for my gas comin' back. But it was a good drive, good to get out in the country."

"Do you go back to the airport after you take us?" Todd asked.

"Not right away, sonny," he said. "Ya see, chances are there's someone at Key Bridge Marriott who's waitin' on a cab. So when I drop your mom and you kids off, and we get your trunks out from the back, someone else'll be right there to take your place. And that's how it goes, all night long."

"Wow," Todd said. I could see him dreaming of what it would be like to drive a taxi for a living. I suddenly feared that he would give up any thoughts of becoming an astronaut and go to taxi school instead. *No!* I wanted to say. *Stop talking! Don't think about it—you've got college and law school. Taxis are for old men with no education!* I wanted to protect Bowser from bad choices, like a concerned and watchful parent.

The Marriott was the fanciest place that we'd ever stayed

in. We shared one room with two beds and one bathroom. Todd slept on the floor in a sleeping bag. I was up early and sneaked out to look for some milk so that we could eat the cereal Mom stashed in her suitcase. I lingered in the hotel souvenir shop a bit too long, trying to sneak a glimpse at the *Penthouse* magazines while the cashier was busy. No such luck. Outside, I found a quart of milk at a convenience store all the way across Key Bridge into Georgetown. I returned to find everyone still asleep. Mom let me be proud that I'd responsibly ventured out on my own for the sake of the family, rather than showing her true feelings: part anger, part alarm.

We spent the first day playing in the pool, waiting for my dad to arrive. I was ready to see the sights, take the Metro, explore the Smithsonian, and see the monuments. For Todd, he may as well have been home at Russ Wagstaff's pool. It was just fun to play for hours and hours. He and Cohleen played Marco Polo and shark and diving for pennies. I was bored with the indoor pool within the first hour, but those two could swim all day.

DC was fascinating for the serious-minded teenager. I feigned boredom with art history that Mom described at the National Museum, but inwardly, I felt an awakening that I recall very distinctly. I would never be the same. In this urban setting, wandering the Smithsonian and the National Mall and then Arlington Cemetery, I recognized my smallness in the world. Not in a discouraging way, but with new excitement for a world of opportunity. Many of our family trips were centered around nature: Yellowstone, Grand Canyon, the California coast. But this was a new experience and so metropolitan. I loved the crowded subway, the buskers, the tailored businessmen, the grungy college students, and the fast-walking, briefcase-carrying men I assumed were politicians. The Lincoln Memorial was incredible, and I felt the power of a nation there like I'd never felt before. A year later, I would become one of the first tenth graders to take advanced placement history, and it was largely due to that DC trip.

"Betcha can't catch that pigeon," Cohleen said. Todd ran after it, and Cohleen laughed her staccato laugh as the gray-purple bird jumped and flew off.

"Would you rather eat pigeon droppings or stand on that street corner in your underwear?" she asked. Fun and games.

That's what it was all about for those two. Cohleen's incessant "would you rather" game and "dare you" contests. She and Todd laughed and played all day long, seemingly ignoring the fact that we were seeing the Apollo 11 command module and the Washington Memorial and the Eternal Flame. Life was just fun for Cohleen, and Todd was the perfect companion.

We drove a rental car up through Pennsylvania Amish country. Todd sat between Cohleen and me in the back, happy to be there and ready to play the alphabet game, Uno, Twenty Questions, I See Something Blue, or any game Cohleen could think of. I wanted to read, or to nap, or to look out the window and ponder. When Mom insisted Todd have a turn sitting by the window, Cohleen and I argued about the squished backseat in the two-door rental car. At one point, we placed a sock between us as a dividing line. But then we argued about whether the edges of the sock were the line and couldn't be touched or the center of the sock was the official divider. Young, toothless, happy Todd just smiled and stayed out of it.

The life-size charcoal drawing of Bowser Todd, hanging eternally in my parents' basement as a lifetime representation of personality, is a smiling six-year-old on a worn-out monster Big Wheel. The Green Hornet Big Wheel was a treasure, and Todd spent endless hours cruising it around the driveway and skidding out down the street. When he was done playing outside or got tired of the rowdy Norris boys interfering with his Big Wheel, he would quietly come inside. Todd loved to scoop himself what Mom called a huge mush bowl of vanilla ice cream after school. He'd take it to the basement and find a comfortable spot on the "puff pillow," a gigantic stuffed pillow chair. I would often find him there watching *The Brady Bunch,* waiting for Cohleen to come home, eager to start a game or to go back outside and ride bikes or to play with anyone who had time for him. "Plays well with others" was his theme.

I didn't have to follow the dog very long after all. After ten minutes of running on a single track through scrub oak, we came to a clearing, where the big dog took a pit stop, much to the dismay of the ponytailed blonde. From there, I found myself behind two big, husky guys, maybe rugby players, who seemed out of place compared with the thin, toned runners I'd seen gathering at the start.

"We bought it at the Mikasa outlet in Park City," Rugby Front said.

"Oh, I love the outlets—we get all our Christmas stuff there," Rugby Rear replied.

"Yeah, since they've expanded, you can find almost anything there."

"And there's that Walmart right next door."

Despite their heavy build and the effeminate conversation, the two kept a fast pace as we climbed the slick serpentine trail. Daylight slowly filled the air, revealing nothing but a cloud completely enveloping us, turning from dark gray to lighter gray. The drops of rain had faded into mist. Occasionally, we'd come to an opening in the trees, a valley overlook where I had to imagine that somewhere out beyond the foggy curtain ten feet in front of me was the view of a city coming to life on this early Saturday morning.

Hope Campground was Aid Station #2, although I don't recall ever seeing or hearing about Aid Station #1. Perhaps that dark human figure pointing up the trail was the official #1. The second was famous for Boy Scouts making pancakes, and while no one was overly fatigued at 5.4 miles and one hour into the race, the novelty of scouts making pancakes for us was an amusing draw, just like old times at Bear River camp. I pictured a dozen Boy Scouts in their decorated green uniforms, a few of them standing at attention with a flag held out, while the remainder were busily flipping hotcakes on the camp stove griddles. Instead, we emerged from scrub oak into a sleepy campground with a few dilapidated camp trailers, their windows dark. We followed a gravel road to the far end of the primitive campground, where a single drippy tarp narrowly covered a picnic table. There were three men griddling pancakes and serving them from a sole aluminum mess kit. One young boy was there, refilling bowls of pretzels and raisins as the runners took handfuls and ran off. No green uniforms. No lineup. No patriotic songs.

I took a pancake, not because I was hungry but just to participate in the whole event that I had read so much about and anticipated. Someone pointed me to a dingy cardboard drop box for headlamps, and while I was glad to be rid of the additional ten ounces bobbling on my head, I wondered if I'd ever see that forty-dollar headlamp again. Then I was given my first half cup of blue Powerade. Little did I know at the time that it was the first of dozens of half cups of blue Powerade that I would consume through the day. Always blue, always divvied up in half cups, which I presume prevented spilling and waste. The race Web site states, *Ten aid stations three to seven miles apart, loaded with all kinds of food and Powerade and water, and even frozen Creamies at AS #6 and the finish and pure strawberry frozen fruit bars at AS #5.* As a novice, I pictured a bottled variety of Powerade and a gourmet lunch spread every couple of hours. But runners are a simple and efficient breed. Most took their half cup and a handful of something—gummy bears, peanuts, Goldfish crackers, granola bar chunks—and moved on quickly.

As I left AS #2, I noticed the beauty of our surroundings. It was completely opposite of what I expected: rocky overlooks, beautiful sunrise, view of the valley as we ascended five thousand vertical feet. Instead, we were tightly enclosed by gray mist, soaking from drips off the deep green pines. There were new June leaves on the aspen, with groves scattered through and interrupting the lofty pine. Thick wide-blade grass covered small meadows, dotted by charcoaled fire circles where summer campers enjoyed the mountains. The trail out of the campground was again a slick muddy track beneath the trees.

It is said that the Eskimos have almost a dozen words for "snow," all different textures and temperature and quality. Leaving the campground, I wondered if there weren't also that many words for "mud." There was the slick slimy kind of mud, a mix of fine dusty silt and small amounts of mist. That was the current mud out of the campground. An hour later, I'd be working out of thick tenacious glue-like mud. And then there was gravel mud, the least bothersome for footing but also the splashiest puddles. Tan-colored clay mud, dark rich soil mud, mud made with snow, mud that swallowed your feet like quicksand, mud hidden under meadows of grass. Like people and their different personalities, every mud had a quality to it. And learning to get along with that quality was a part of the long day, just like discovering and getting along with new friends. Enjoying mud, even, for the benefits offered: cool, not dry and dusty, gives fertile ground for new life. The mud-people analogy got in my head as runners started to separate on the trail a little more. And it got me thinking of my brothers and sisters, their differences, their qualities, and the blessings of growing up in a large family together.

My fellow runners tried to use the shoulders of the trail, but the grass was equally slick, and tall enough to blind their footing. Most had given up an attempt to maintain dry feet, slogging through mud puddles as if they were nonexistent. I was still fairly conservative, avoiding puddles not only for the sake of my white shoes but also to hope for relatively dry feet. I tried to gain traction on knobby roots in the narrow trail, but they too were slick, and I often stumbled to my knees. Only a few miles into the race, the last thing I needed was a knee injury.

Allen family knees. In her nineties, Grandma Allen had bad knees, huge knobby protuberant knees poking out from a wheelchair. My dad had arthroscopic knee surgery in his fifties, and while his injury was totally unrelated to his mother's arthritis, still it seemed obvious that "the family has bad knees." Chris had always suffered from knee problems; his first major surgery in the seventies was just a short time before the less-invasive arthroscopy became the norm. My knees have held out. I was a mogul skier, preferring the big bumps to powder or groomed snow. I could run and had recently finished my first marathon. I could climb a mountain, and then run down, pounding my knees with each footfall and feeling only minimal inflammatory heat and pain later in the day, fully recovered by the next. But I had the constant fear that I would indeed inherit the family knee troubles. And somewhere in my training the prior month, I started to notice a click in my right knee, as I'd tried to tell Dr. Scholl. Not painful, but just a little click that wasn't right. I wore an elastic wrap on that knee for the race, not for support (I'm of the opinion that wraps provide no support) but for increased awareness of the knee so that I would be extra cautious. Slipping through mud and tree roots and a deep rutted trail, I started to worry.

Bowser has the worst knee story. As a teenager, he was an all-around athlete: basketball, soccer, biking, running, skiing. He was a super active kid, always willing to join a pick-up game or go on a last-minute hike. Then during his fifteenth summer, his life changed forever. It was at the Bennion Boys Ranch, a two-month summer work camp situated at a horse ranch in Idaho. My parents thought the ranch and the dorm living would be ideal for Todd's otherwise lazy summer, and it was his second season there. After morning chores were done and lunch was cleaned up, the boys were out in the sagebrush field playing Capture the Flag. Todd was a natural, grown out of his little-boy body and into a muscular man's frame. But he was no match for the big gopher hole hiding beneath the sage. Just that quickly, he'd snapped a major ligament, and life would never be the same.

Todd underwent surgical repair and rehabilitation. But basically, he was told to give up competitive sports forever, and that if he wanted to preserve his knee, he would always need to be careful. I remember him later writing an essay for college on the assignment "What is the most significant thing that's happened in your life?" He titled it simply, "My Knee."

If Bowser was a nice person before, knee surgery made him extraordinary. By his senior year in high school, he was a popularity magnet, not as a jock or a great student leader but as a friendly, good dude. He was full of compassion. He was even-tempered. He related to young and old, unintimidated by and unintimidating to anyone. He was charitable and caring, an ideal missionary to the people of Chile at age nineteen. Always well loved as the youngest in the family, now he was well loved as a warm, friendly, good-natured adult. His best friend was a little person. The elderly neighbors who thought that my teenage friends were evil gang members instead knew my little brother Todd as a saint. He was a buddy, not just to Cohleen but to everyone. Bowser the beloved pet became Bowser all over again.

Todd was my only younger brother, and while I sought attention and admiration from everyone, little brother was top of my list. I wanted him to look up to me as the "oldest" of the younger half of the family, as much or more than I looked up to my big brothers. I wanted to be cool in his eyes and to do things that he couldn't do.

"No way will you dive off of there," Todd said to me.

"What'll you give me?" I replied, spurring him on. "How about a shaved ice?" Everything was a challenge or a bet in our family, even though my parents were never the type to bet or gamble. It was the way we interacted, daring each other to do great or foolish things.

"I'll clean your bike for a week," he said.

"Ooh, nice one. It's really muddy right now." The Mongoose BMX was still my pride and joy, though often set aside now with the Yamaha 125 motorcycle I'd purchased.

Todd and I swam in a beautiful pool of water in Waiamea Gardens on the island of Oahu. Thirty feet above us towered several tiers of green mossy cliffs. The Polynesian men had performed beautiful dives from thirty and even fifty feet, and then welcomed the audience to jump in the cool fresh water and enjoy the waterfalls. Only a few of us jumped in, while the rest of the family enjoyed flowered-scented scenic trails through the park.

Taking the challenge, I made my way up the falls to a heavily treed trail around the backside of the cliffs. Todd was seven and watched eagerly and with disbelief as I climbed the same trail as the great divers. While he knew I could dive at the local swimming pool, thirty feet above a small Hawaiian pond was entirely different. I knew from Scout camp at Lake Powell that I could do the dive and would have readily accepted the dare without a shaved ice or bike washing reward.

Reaching the precipice, I smiled down at Todd, and then eyed the beautiful view of Waiamea beach. In September, the northwest shore would sport some of the highest waves and top surfers in the world. But it was hard to imagine in June, when just a small white surf lapped into the white sands. A few sunbathers and families came out this way, but most were an hour away in the Waikiki area. I could see my parents on a nearby trail but purposely didn't call attention to my death-defying dive. The sun was high, reflecting on the water below and causing Todd and me to squint at one another. There was little brother, Bowser Todd. He looked up at me with some disbelief and lots of apprehension. I felt like pounding my chest or at least flexing my muscles, like a superhero about to swoop down and save a seven-year-old from some unseen evil. I wished he didn't have to squint to see me, as I wanted him to see the boldness on my face, the lack of fear, the pride that I felt in being his big brother.

"You ready?" I yelled down. The sound echoed and caught the attention of others around the pond.

"Be careful," Todd replied. He wanted to let me out of

the wager but didn't know how to express it. He sat nervously picking at moss on a large flat rock.

I picked up some dirt and dropped it down on the water, just the way I'd learned to drip water down at the Swim and Tennis Club. It gave you a sense of how far the water was and how much falling time there would be. It was a long drop, almost twice the height of a high dive at the club. Mom would shriek if she saw me that high. Normally, I might have panicked, too, but with Todd watching, I felt powerfully daring.

"Here goes!" With that, I crossed my arms on my chest, bent my knees slightly, and then jumped outward. The fall was immense and fast. I watched the water carefully, its shimmering glint coming at me very quickly. I kept my legs close together and toes pointed, knowing what a hard splash it would be otherwise. By halfway down, my arms went outward, swinging to keep my balance. Then suddenly, I splashed in. My pointed feet curved me backward, bringing my chin down hard on the water. My hands and arms also clapped down and started stinging immediately. It was not graceful, and rising from the cloud of bubbles in the water, I realized how foolish the high jump was. But I was alive, and my arms and legs were all working, and my neck wasn't hurt. And I was happy. I lunged up out of the water and shook my long hair.

"Ha-ha! Pretty cool, huh?"

"You're crazy," Todd said.

"You told me to do it!" I said jokingly.

"Don't do it again," he entreated.

The cliff jump had the wrong effect on Todd. I did it to impress him, but it just scared him. He peered around nervously, as if looking for Cohleen to come and swim with us and ease the tension I'd caused. He was almost ready to cry.

"Okay, no more cliff jumping," I said. "Let's go under the falls."

We swam across the pool and showered under one of the minor falls, and then climbed up behind the larger waterfall. The noise of the pounding water was deafening, but the mossy wet cave was fascinating. We stuck our arms out through the falls, feeling the massive weight of water hammering down.

"Incredible!" I yelled to him. He nodded his head, slightly nervous that I was going to try something foolish again, like jumping out through the falls. I backed away into the cave, and we both sat wordless for a few minutes.

Hawaii was a dream vacation for our family. Unlike many recent family vacations, the whole family was able to go to Hawaii, even our three grandparents. And in typical Allen fashion, we were far removed from the high-rises and nightlife of Waikiki. We lived in a rented house in Laie, a residential neighborhood near the college, over a mile from the beach. It was a professor's house, cheaply sublet to us while his family vacationed to Utah. It was a typical Hawaiian house: windows with no screens or curtains, cockroaches and geckos freely roaming the floor and ceiling, and wood furniture always moist and sticky. But despite the digs, Hawaii was the ultimate holiday, the most memorable in twenty-plus years of family vacations.

While many days were filled with expeditions to local sites such as Waiamea, much of our time was empty. The adults read, napped, explored the campus, and visited people that Chris knew from his missionary experience there. The youngest three, with me at the head, were bored. We were in the greatest place on earth, and we complained of boredom.

"Go to the beach!" Mom finally advised.

I found a BMX bike that fit me in the garage. It was my opinion that anything left out or unlocked must have been okay for us to use. No bikes for Cohleen and Todd, though. They walked, toting towels, a boogie board, and sand buckets. Todd's nose was covered with a thick layer of white zinc oxide. He wore a Piutes hat, a Little League hand-me-down of Bryan's. He was short-haired and scrawny. Cohleen was twelve, still a girl but quickly becoming a young woman. Her hair was long and black from an early age. She wore Kmart sunglasses and a new flowered sarong she'd bought at the Polynesian Cultural Center. I rode circles around them as we slowly made our way to Pounders Beach.

"No way!" was Cohleen's first reaction to the waves as we got closer.

Pounders was a popular beach for locals but not for tourists. The name came from the steepness of the sand, which caused the six-foot waves to suddenly fold and crash down rather than slowly curling over. Anything under that crash, man or animal, was pounded hard into the sand.

"Looks fun," I said.

"No way are you going to go in those waves," she replied.

"They're not that big," I said. A couple of teenage local boys were bodysurfing in the big waves, and half a dozen other locals sat in rickety lawn chairs on the beach. No one paid any attention to us as we dropped our towels near the high water mark on the sand. They knew that we were misdirected tourists who would soon discover why Pounders was for locals only.

"Come on, Bowser!" I yelled over the noise of crashing surf. I had stripped down to my swimsuit in one quick motion and was headed toward the water. It wasn't our first ocean experience, and I knew that I could at least jump through the waves and swim on the ocean side of them if they were too big to surf on. Bowser hesitated with a clear look of concern on his face. He looked to Cohleen to see what she was going to do.

"Well, I'm going to build a castle," Cohleen said with a rural twang, like a farmer needing to get to work. "See if those waves are big enough to knock over my castle." She took one bucket and left the other for Bowser to pick up. He looked from me to her several times.

"Come on, Bowse-man, let's get in the water!" I tried again to convince him to join me. This scene was all too familiar to us, not in ocean waves but in every other aspect of our lives: playing Monopoly, hiking, skiing, shopping. I wanted to be Todd's hero and have him be my little brother buddy. If a dog was man's best friend, I hoped Bowser would be mine. But Cohleen was always there between us, closer in age, much more fun, a lifelong companion. Bowser always chose her over me. My big brother show-off adventures failed to capture the little guy's esteem, but Cohleen's game-time exuberance never disappointed. He smiled and waved me off, saying something polite that I couldn't hear. Then he picked up the bucket and joined Cohleen digging in wet sand.

I stood and let the cool ocean water come up to my ankles, and then my knees. I stared out beyond the surf to a distant curved horizon and listened to the loud sucking noises that the retreating waves made. The cool mist was refreshing after a hot, sticky bike ride through the neighborhood. I thought for a long time about being alone in the company of others, wishing I could get my little brother, Bowser the puppy dog, to be my buddy. I must not be a good buddy. I had friends, a large family, and a good life. But I was not a good buddy. I stared out at the sky and the water and wondered what would become of my life.

Chapter 3: My Big Sister Diana, and Snow

Long after the Boy Scouts and the campground, we emerged from the trees onto a gravel road that cut south around the mountainside. Stable gravel footing was a welcome relief from the slick mud trail, and I pounded and scraped my shoes to get the mud off. The road brought our first set of spectators, half a dozen people holding umbrellas and shouting words of encouragement. Unlike most city marathons, the trail race is notably absent of spectators. A few volunteers greet you at each aid station, and a few faithful family members gather in the spots where the appointed trail crosses accessible roads. But we were otherwise alone with each other, the hours marked only by a slight change of terrain or change of weather.

We stayed on the road for only a few hundred feet, and then veered off to intersecting trails, more dirt roads, and trails ascending through dense scrub. Perhaps the only bit of helpful information from the dinner and orientation meeting the previous night was that bright orange ribbon would occasionally mark a straight trail and that orange and blue together marked a turn of route. Often separated by entire visual fields from anyone else, and foggy as it was, I was grateful for these few ribbon markers to guide me. And it wasn't long before I was grateful for footprints in the snow.

I should have known it would snow. There were mist and rain at 5,000 feet of elevation, cool temperatures for June, and fog atop the mountain. I pulled from my pocket the tiny piece of paper on which I'd copied the elevation graph and made estimates on mileage. I guessed that we had ascended 2,500 feet, or just over half the climb to Kolob Basin Overlook. After the overlook—if there was an overlook through fog—we would rapidly descend over 3,000 feet to a point that was almost halfway. Then the whole thing started over again: climb, fall, hike, run. As the rain turned thick and slushy, and then white snow started to accumulate on the trail, I seriously questioned my judgment on leaving the jacket behind. My long-sleeve shirt was soaked through, and my socks and shoes were muddy and wet. I tied a bandana around my head, a "lid on my top" to keep warm, as Grandma said. But the wet snow stuck to my face, chest, and thighs, keeping me thoroughly chilled. The only way out, the only way to stay warm, was to run.

I am a winter runner. I'm invigorated by running through cold and snow and had done lots of it prior to Squaw Peak. Running in the heat is immediately bothersome to me, and I usually take a couple of months off each summer for that reason. But in cold, snowy weather, there's an increased desire to push on, to warm up through movement and muscle use. I recall running one very snowy afternoon across Twentieth East, and then down Thirty-ninth South toward the hospital. Cars splashed me with slush as they drove by. The wind pelted snow at me from the west, and my front was entirely covered with icy white when I arrived at the hospital doors. I stepped into the surgeon's lounge as an unrecognizable hooded figure, dripping ice and rapidly melting in the warm indoors. The too-hot shower burned my cheeks and toes, but I basked in its warmth for a long, long time. The contrast is enlivening: to be so cold and wet, and then so warm and comfortable; to be so hungry, and then to binge on endless calories of food and drink.

Winter running is also amazingly quiet. On January mornings, I would run up Millcreek Canyon, where traffic was so rare, I could make tracks through the snow in the middle of the road. The falling snow absorbed every sound, and the narrow canyon enveloped me in silent darkness. I once ran right into a skunk and luckily escaped without stink. I often found myself overdressed and would peel off layers, leaving pieces by the roadside as I ascended and warmed up, and then picking them up as I ran down the canyon.

Squaw Peak was different, though. There was no warm shower to return to in an hour. I was soaked through and would remain so for another ten hours, if I made it that far. Threads of doubt weaved their way into my thoughts on the otherwise quiet trail. Two to three inches now covered the trail, falling fast enough to almost fill and cover the footprints of those before me. Rain and wet I could handle, assuming the temperature was not too chilly. The long day I could manage, just as I had trained and prepared for. But snow was unexpected.

The snow took me back to my first day skiing at a ski

resort, during a horrible blizzard in Park City, Utah. I had learned to ski on the golf course hills behind our Wasatch Drive home. My brothers built ski jumps and took snapshots of each other flying off. With borrowed boots and skis, much too large for me, I joined the brothers in marching up the hill. The slope was mild, sufficient for sledding but barely enough for skiing. I could ski straight down without turning, snowplowing, or slowing down until the flat bottom would naturally stop me. I even tried the smaller jumps, splattering down on to the soft snow without injury and ready to do it again.

At seven, I was ready to ski for real, or at least I'd begged my parents to let me try. The opportunity arose for Diana to take me with a group of her friends. It was clear that I was more of a chaperone for her at sixteen rather than a ski partner; nevertheless, we were both grateful for the opportunity. Diana was the oldest in the family, the "queen," the big sister, the boss, the second mother. Without prior parenting experience, Mom and Dad were overly concerned about Diana's involvement with boys or with friends of questionable nature. At a young age, I watched their careful regulation of her, arguing about curfew time, discussing which boys were appropriate to date, and frequently battling her use of time. The Park City trip was almost more of a punishment for Diana. "Yes, you can go skiing with your friends, but you have to take your little brother along and teach him how to ski." I can only imagine her real reaction to this penalty, but toward me, she showed nothing but interest and excitement.

This is the hardest chapter to write. Not because of the snow, although both Park City and thirty-two years later on Squaw Peak were agonizing snow experiences. Not because of any impending tragedy or accident. But only because Diana is hard to write about. She was a second mother to me, and mothers are those whom we have the strongest feelings for. Strong feelings of love, sentiments indescribable, longing for nurture. But these feelings are mingled with perplexing negative ones, tensions, and resentment for the strong hand of guidance—guidance that was ultimately rewarding but momentarily troublesome. A college writing professor advised me never to write about my mother or my wife. "Those things which are still emotionally very present for us do not allow for good writing perspective," he said. And Mother would always be emotionally present. I once offered him a story about lying to my mom, and then traveling to Canada to visit Elizabeth. He glanced at it briefly, and then threw it out and asked me to go back to writing about my missionary work in Taiwan, my high school stories, and my childhood memories. My mother is indirectly part of all of these stories and memories, yet rarely can I focus directly on her. And Diana is not far off, difficult to write about.

Big sisters are a mix of nurturing love and harsh bossiness. With parental caring, Diana would enter my dark bedroom late at night after her shift at Jolley's Drug. She caressed my hair—she loved my long thick "Dutch Boy" hair—and sometimes kissed me good night. On the dresser the next morning, I would find a paper sack of goodies, Tootsie Rolls, Swedish fish, and Twizzlers. For my birthday, she gave me a yellow T-shirt that read *I love Salt Lake* on it, and despite being my least favorite color, the shirt quickly took the place of favorite over my purple Bubble Yum shirt. Diana organized family photos, knowing how those memories would be meaningful to us someday. Once when my parents were out of town, she drove us up the canyon to later surprise Mom and Dad with family photos in the setting of beautiful fall leaves. She was ever thoughtful, considering the effects of scrapbooks, photos, and life experiences now that would be meaningful in the future. She seemed to be very aware that there was a future as adults, as if she could see all of us in twenty years: adults, parents, uncles, and aunts gathered together to celebrate Thanksgiving, old fuddy-duddies to the next generation, talking about old times, reminiscing with photos, helping each other through hard times. I don't remember *seeing* that as a child or a teenager, and not until I had several of my own children did I realize that it had happened. But Diana saw it all along and was preparing us for it.

At the same time, Diana could say things that "only a mother" would say: "Tuck in your shirt," "Your hair looks bad," and "Eat your peas—or else." She wanted us to be upright citizens and would not hesitate to tell us if our clothes were out of style or our actions were distasteful. Even as a teenager with her own typical child-parent conflicts, Diana ironically defended Mom and Dad and would not allow us to back talk or mock them. She again saw the future, that someday in their aging years, we would all regret the trouble we'd caused Mom and Dad as kids.

Diana is center stage in everyone's home movies, often controlling or arranging the scene, bopping Chris on the head, yanking Dave around, giving the eye to Bryan for slouching. "Diana Banana" never quite fit as a nickname in a family bent on nicknames. Banana implying fun, squishy, yellow, and sweet. I still occasionally hear her called Banana, now almost fifty years old, when someone wants to interact playfully with her. But it is unnatural for me, like the disrespect and unbefitting name, "Sandy," that some have inappropriately used for my mother, Sandra. Some people in our lives are more endeared by their proper name and title, not by a nickname.

Diana worked hard. From early teen years, we remember big sister Diana going to work almost as regularly and steadfastly as Dad. We visited her at the zoo, where her minimum-wage job was barely enough to justify the time away from homework. She worked at Trolley Square Ice Cream, a noisy, crowded, old-fashioned sit-down ice cream parlor at the heart of the upscale mall. She treated us to banana splits, perhaps in honor of the nickname some wanted her to fit. We watched in awe as the party table next to ours received the "Kitchen Sink," some fifty scoops of various flavors served in a real sink-like dish and smothered in toppings. Everyone grabbed a spoon and dug in, ignoring the fact that they shared spitty spoonfuls. Diana worked at Jolley's Drug as a cashier; her best friend, Jodi Jolley, was a part of the family business. She spent a summer working at Jackson Lake Lodge. I remember pulling in the Signal Mountain campground, where she was saving a spot for our camper. She wore a light blue JLL shirt and had short brown hair. She smiled and waved us down as Dad drove the cumbersome camper into the narrow campsite. She was an adult. I had seen it since early childhood but now recognized it more than ever. My big sister, having lived alone most of the summer, was an adult.

The day arrived for our ski trip, and I was up early with excitement and trepidation. We rode to Park City in a friend's car and arrived by late morning. I was the novelty of the day, the seven-year-old cute little brother who was skiing for the first time. It was all new to me: trudging in ski boots from the parking lot to the hill, buying a sticker ticket and attaching it with a metal wire, watching as skiers schussed down the steepest hill I'd ever seen. I wore a brown knit cap that was mine, but everything else was a hand-me-down: goggles with yellow lenses, red ski parka, red bib-style snow pants, and blue down mittens. And of course I had the Allen family requisite bandana tied around my face and neck like a cowboy bandit.

The blizzard came early. Snow pelted down on us as we suited up. The packed snow on my boots made it difficult to put my skis on, and Diana and I fumbled for several minutes, trying to click into the bindings and then attach the safety straps. I was anxious to ski on a real ski hill, but also terrified by the conditions: snow falling so thick that I could barely make out the First Time chairlift we were walking toward. Diana had said a temporary good-bye to her friends, assuming we'd catch up to them later and that she might even get a few runs with them. I knew it was hard for her to watch them walk toward the gondola while she was stuck with me on the bunny hill.

It was a hard day. Everything was hard for me. The chairlift moved faster than I expected, and I almost didn't get on. The chairs were covered in snow and felt dangerously slippery suspending me twenty feet off the ground. I was totally immersed in snow, already cold when we reached the top of the first run. And then there was skiing to be done. I struggled to make it down the five-foot little hill where you step off at the top of the chairlift. This was not what I was used to at my home golf course hill.

"We'll do a couple here, and then move up to Payday!" Diana shouted through the storm.

"I can't move," I replied, trying to lift my skis and walk through several inches of sticky powder.

"Just like you've learned, slide, and then snowplow!" she yelled. "Snowplow, snowplow, snowplow—that's the most important thing, to slow down and to turn." I could hear my dad in her voice, always teaching caution and care. Caution with money. Caution in bad weather. Caution in life decisions.

"Okay," I said. I wanted to be brave. I was a natural at this. I had started on skis earlier than any of my four older siblings. I was the prodigy. I was going to be taking jumps and burning down the mountain by midday. So why was I so terrified that I couldn't even move?

"Come on, here we go." Diana started down the hill ahead of me. I made as wide a snowplow as possible, and then shuffled forward an inch at a time. The hill was twice as steep as anything I'd been on.

"I can't move!" I complained. Now there was a whine in my voice, and even I could hear my own fright.

"Back and forth, come on!" There was frustration and regret in her voice. If I couldn't even step off the top of the easiest hill, how would she ever catch up to her friends?

"It's too steep!"

"Back and forth, not straight down. It's not like the golf course hill."

"I can't!" Now she was side-stepping up the hill to get me, and it was not without anger in her brusque marching steps.

"Come on, we've got to get down off the top," she said.

With all my might, I aimed my skis toward her and scootched forward, and then started sliding. A wide snowplow brought me to an abrupt stop again. Then I tried it again, moving slightly and slowly forward. As soon as I felt the smallest amount of speed, I dropped to the ground near her skis.

"That's good," she said. "You've got to know how to fall down."

"I'm good at falling," I said, trying to lighten up the trouble that I was sure to be in.

"Back and forth," she said. "Don't aim your skis downhill. Just ski over to that pole, and then turn and go over to …" She looked for something to aim for. "Look over toward that tower."

"What tower?" I said. I could barely make out the clock tower above the ticket office, but I wanted to emphasize to her how severe the weather was.

"Come on, I'll help you up," she said. I popped up easily, but with my skis pointing downhill, I immediately started going too fast again. I dropped to my bum a few yards down the hill. One ski popped off as I tumbled over. I could sense the exasperation as Diana skied down to help me again.

"Back and forth," she emphasized. "Ski across the hill, not down it."

We were almost an hour getting down that first run. I was covered with snow from frequent falls and the blizzard refusing to let up. The hill was barren except for the two of us, and I wondered if that was normal for such a well-known resort. At the bottom, the "liftie" kept busy shoveling snow from the boarding area and was ready with a broom to sweep off our chair when it came around.

"I could go in the lodge for a while," I offered. Diana thought for a moment. I'm sure she pondered the effects of either scenario. If I went in the lodge and she left me, would my parents find out and accuse her of abandoning me? If I didn't go in the lodge, she was sure to get zero skiing in for herself.

"No, let's do it again," she said. "You'll do better. Just snowplow, back and forth." She made wide sweeping gestures with her arms. "I know you can do better—just like on the golf course."

The second time up was, unfortunately, no better than the first. As if the storm could get worse, our visibility was now zero as the heavy snow continued. I was frigid cold, especially my toes and fingers. I continued to fall, get up, get scared, fall again. Halfway down the hill, I gave up.

"I just can't do it!" I cried. "I can't see through the snow." The bandana over my mouth and nose was wet and icy, muffling my voice. But she didn't need to hear me. She knew we were finished.

"Take off your skis," she said. I popped out of the bindings without questioning her. "You take my poles, and I'll carry your skis down." I picked up my skis and wrapped them together with the safety strap, and then we swapped. It was the beginning of a long tradition of the same: the adult carries both skis, and the child carries both poles. I began walking down the hill, Diana skiing with my skis in her arms just ahead of me. The storm had beat us, or at least beat me. I was a disappointment to my big sister and kept her from enjoying the day with her friends. I thought I'd never ski again.

The cafeteria was packed with people and very noisy. The room smelled of deep frying, charbroiled burgers, and sweaty wet wool. We had no money to buy anything at the expensive resort and instead were directed to some small rooms in the basement where "brown baggers" hung out. Diana was surprised to find her friends there.

"It's closed, it's all closed," the blonde girl said excitedly.

"Huh?" Diana asked.

"We tried to get on the gondola," the brunette answered, "but they said it was too windy. We skied on Payday twice, but they said everything was closing."

"No way!" Diana said.

"John said the highway is even closed," the blonde said. "We're stuck up here!"

"How'd you do, little guy?" the brunette asked me. I didn't know what to say. Ice melted and dripped off my knit cap. My nose was running, and I wiped it with a sweater sleeve.

"He did well," Diana responded, patting me on the back. "We did two runs and then came in."

"One and a half runs," I corrected her, embarrassed by my failure.

"Well, that's good!" brunette said. "You'll be on Jupiter Bowl before you know it." Diana smiled, proud of me. The irritation was gone. The frustration, which I thought had ruined my standing with my big sister forever, was gone. I was okay. I would ski again, and I would ski well.

We spent the next several hours huddled into small rooms, awaiting news about the highway. Boisterous groups of teenage boys played cards and teased flirtatious girls. The interactions were new to me. I'd never really seen Diana that way. She watched over me, but from a distance, as she talked, posed, glanced, flirted, and smiled. As darkness set in, I was absolutely starving and could feel the exhaustion causing my face to scowl, almost to tears. At that moment, my big sister did something for me that I've never ever forgotten. She brought me half of a double chocolate doughnut.

"Brad is dedicating this to your first day of skiing," she said.

"Brad?" I asked. She pointed to a boy with long blond hair sitting at the far end of another table. He was smiling my way, holding up half a doughnut as if in cheers to me.

"Where's yours?" I asked.

"Come on, it's yours," she said. "I know you're starving, and I didn't think we'd be up here this late."

"It's not your fault the roads are closed," I defended.

"Just enjoy it," she retorted. "I think we're going to be rescued soon."

Enjoy it I did. Slowly, delectably, my tears turning to happiness from despair. I've never had a more appreciated morsel in all my life. I saw Diana not as the source of my despair, but as my caretaker in a time of great need. I was so grateful for her motherly attention. I have relished double chocolate doughnuts since that day and still stop at Dan's Grocery once a week to indulge.

Within thirty minutes, my dad was there to pick us up in the Chevrolet Bel Air. I sensed tension between he and Diana, and I'm sure she felt responsible for the failed day. Failed skiing and a stormy highway mess that must have called for some white-knuckled driving for Dad. But, as I would learn in years to come, that tension was in fact not blame or anger, but genuine concern and worry. Mom was so glad to have us home again, but this was also expressed in apparent sighs of anger rather than joyful hugs or adulation. I would not ski another time until the following season when Dad could personally take me up to Snowbird and, on a beautiful sunny day, guide me down the easy Chickadee run over and over.

There was the slightest amount of view over Kolob Basin. It was shocking, in fact, to suddenly catch glimpses of far-off green farms in the valley below. The heavy clouds were moving up the mountain and occasionally parted to show our altitude. I have no fear of heights but was dizzied by the sensation of coming out of a fog and unexpectedly being so high above the valley floor. The blizzard was gone, but now a bit of wind kicked up from the south and gave my wet body an uncomfortable chill.

Just a mile later was Camel Pass. I'd run sixteen miles through rain, mud, snow, and fog. I'd shared greetings with one or two fellow runners but otherwise climbed alone along unfamiliar mountain trails marked with sporadic orange and blue ribbons. I'd gulped several half cups of blue Powerade, snatched some raisins and gummy bears, and munched on handfuls of pretzels moistened by snowflakes and dripping sweat. It was only 9:00 AM, four hours into the fifty-mile expedition that I expected would take me at least twelve.

To my surprise, a truck had somehow found its way up through the snow to Camel Pass. The camper-top truck held my first drop bag, a useless stash of sunscreen, carbohydrate gel, and a baseball cap. But next to the truck was a welcome sight: a large canvas camping tent. After discarding my drop bag, I entered the tent and found the same small table of drinks and goodies, a man and his wife pleasantly welcoming us, and a small crowd of five or six runners shivering wet and hunched over in the five-foot-high shelter. It was a tiny space for runners to move and stay warm, but they shivered, shook, paced, stretched, and donned dry jackets from their drop bags.

    I was hungry. Not overwhelmingly so, and even after four hours I could tell I was still excited with the rush of accomplishing my goal. But the tinge of hunger made me realize that I was already falling behind on the caloric needs. I chose for my midmorning snack bananas dipped in peanut butter, peanuts, grapes, and Ritz crackers. I also refilled the two twenty-ounce hydration bottles on my waist pack. In one I poured my homemade mix of pink lemonade, sugar, salt, and potassium. In the other, a "recovery drink" with protein and electrolytes. I was worried that my sudden influx of protein and fat would discomfit me with cramps, but it was necessary at this juncture in the endurance run, and the three-thousand-foot descent that I was about to begin was a good time to build up energy stores again. I was less than five minutes in the tent when it started to get crowded and uncomfortable. I stepped out into the cold, looked east toward clearing skies, and started running downhill.

    Social isolation was certainly not a pattern in my life but was becoming a trend. Reviewing my history of activities and involvement, one would think that I was extremely gregarious. I was student body president of both my elementary and high schools. I dated and never missed a school dance, whether girl's choice or my own selection. My scrapbook is loaded with dance photos, groups of friends acting funny, decorating the school for Spirit Week, and doing gymnastics in front of huge crowds as a cheerleader. Now, at almost forty, my colleagues could not fathom that I once led cheers in front of football stadium crowds. I am not shy or introverted but certainly conservative in my communication and friendliness. And in the years of becoming a runner, I had always run alone: never trained with a buddy and never joined a Saturday morning group run. Now I was in a long-distance run with two hundred others and had yet to speak to anyone.

I was reminded of Diana the socialite. It was Diana that paved the way for her younger siblings in a lifestyle of socializing and popularity. Nothing out of the ordinary, perhaps, but new to all of us as we watched her become a social teenager. The whole scene was fascinating to me as an eight-year-old. Three teenage boys wearing tuxedo tops and boxer shorts, standing on the doorstep, serenading Diana as one of them asked her to prom. A loud and crowded gymnasium; I held tightly to Dad's hand as we found Diana smiling, laughing, screaming in delight with girlfriends celebrating another East High Leopard basketball win. Early morning, squealy, scantily clad friends "kidnapping" Diana from her yellow bedroom to surprise her with birthday breakfast at Village Inn. My first-time parents agonized in late nights, boyfriends, studies pushed aside, and the reckless joy of late teen years. Young Cohleen and I marveled at what our futures might hold, amazed by the freedom and joy of a driver's license and a job and awed by the split personality of our eldest sister, gleeful and carefree with friends but typical teenage grumpy and insolent at home.

Like it was yesterday, I well recall being used as a Christmas elf to ask Christian Johnson to the Christmas dance. Christian was her first true love, and his name has never entirely faded from family conversation. On a cold snowy late-November night, she persuaded me with extra Jolley Drug penny candy to dress as an elf, sing a little jingle, and creatively query Christian's availability for the upcoming dance. My pajamas, similar to Robin Williams on *Mork and Mindy*, suited perfect for the occasion. They were tight-fitting green and red long underwear. A pair of moccasins, a red felt belt, and a green pointed cap with a bell on top. She wrapped a three-by-three-foot box with decorative paper and a giant bow on top, and then placed me inside the box. I remember the feeling of being cramped in that box in the cold weather on a stranger's porch, wondering if they would ever answer the doorbell and knowing that I was about to greatly embarrass myself. All for a few extra Tootsie Rolls, and the winning approval of my seventeen-year-old sister. A few days later, he said "yes," in a much less creative but equally effective manner, and I therefore considered my humiliating exploit a great success.

Not to suggest that Diana wasn't a good student; in fact, she received a full scholarship to the university. She was an outstanding student and also worked many hours at part-time jobs starting at age fourteen. But she burned the candle at both ends with dates, dances, Pep Club, ball games, boys, girlfriend parties, music, and what seemed to a naive little brother, an insatiable avarice for fun and popularity. One of the most common phrases heard at our house was, "Diana, get off the phone!"

I say "popularity," but I never felt it as a negative trait. Diana was not and is not a social climber for society's sake. Her popularity was not for power over others or prestige in light of others. She was not mean-spirited, though I witnessed the tears and soap opera caused by the callousness of others: backbiting, boyfriend stealing, a black rose left on the doorstep. Diana was simply a gregarious and outgoing person. She had inherited Dad's geeky-square class-president gumption and Mom's deep and soft friendly compassion and mixed them into a confident, outgoing, joyful, fresh, fun-loving young woman. She started a trend for, and perhaps a need for, popularity and involvement, which the Allen children would closely follow.

Diana attended a New Year's Eve party at my house a few years ago. A couple of her children came and played board games with mine, but her husband stayed home with two sick kids. It was an "open house" type party, and we'd casually invited neighbors, old friends, and family to join us for as much or as little time as they wanted. Diana was amazing, and a significant asset for our not-so-well-attended gathering. In just a few minutes of talking with people, she brought together distant connections, paid great compliments, and played the well-liked hostess role like I could have never done.

"I'm Rich's sister Diana," she introduced herself to new neighbors we'd never spoken to.

"Randy Brady," the man replied, not terribly pleasant. "This is my wife, Colleen, and my three daughters. We've just moved in on Kempner."

"Kempner—that's the street that borders the creek?" Diana asked.

"I think so, but we're on the *other* side of the street, away from the creek," he replied.

"But it's such a great neighborhood—I often wish we'd moved over here," she told him. "I helped Rich find this house, and I almost wish we'd taken it ourselves."

"Well, we're in a bit of a fixer-upper, but so far, we like it."

"I knew Terry Brady at East High—did you grow up here?" she asked.

"That's my uncle! And Colleen went to East, but I grew up in Granger," Randy replied.

"I'm sure you're ten years younger that I am," Diana said to Colleen, "but it's the same old East High. Were you from the avenues or the zoo area?"

In minutes, the Bradys were welcomed into our home, as Diana discovered Randy's job in insurance, Colleen's recent graduation from law school, and Uncle Terry's whereabouts. For me, that was about as far as I could take an awkward conversation. But an hour later, I discovered Diana still talking with the Bradys and having welcomed two other couples into the conversation. She has a talent that is remarkable to me, rivaled only by my mother, who can befriend the plumber and know his whole life story before the drain is repaired.

I've often reflected on the way Diana's popularity shaped my own and how they contrast. Diana sought fun and involvement. I'm much less fun and often find myself seeking instead for prestige and notoriety. She wanted to be part of the group, sharing in merriment. I want to lead the group and be seen by them as the chief. She respects and builds others in socializing with them, while I compete with others and want to be better than them. Diana could ski with a group and have fun or ski alone and enjoy being out on the mountain. I like skiing with a group because I'm usually the best skier and could never ski alone because there would be no one to watch me.

Our differences became apparent when I was seventeen and intent on winning a school election. Diana was the expert to turn to, with both the artistic abilities to make posters and the social know-how to compose a winning campaign. She had finished college and was working part time on a masters degree while employed by the university department of student services. She was busy, lived with roommates in a duplex about half a mile away from us, and was desperately feeling ostracized in Utah as an unmarried twenty-five-year-old woman. When Mom went to her with a request to help with my campaign, she was reluctant but willing to use her talents and put in the many hours it would require.

We approached it differently from the start and ended up with a mixed conglomerate of posters and presentations. Diana wanted me to be seen as one of the people, to say, "Hey, I'm one of you." I wanted to be seen as a leader, to say, "Hey, I'm better than you." I took the advice of a politically savvy neighbor, who said that every photo of me should be in a suit and tie, looking like the man who should be president. At the same time, Diana designed a poster called "The Making of a President," showing ten photos of me growing up, my first bicycle, first date, getting a driver's license, et cetera. It was the "Hey, I'm one of you" theme, with the message that I'd be a good president because I'm a good, solid nice guy. But my first appearance in the primary election took a very different approach. It was a video compilation, which I had done all myself, showing clips of me as a cheerleader, me doing a high school television ad, me in a suit and tie doing work at a desk. It was all about showing that I was the man for president because I was already there.

I narrowly squeezed through the primaries, despite the tension I'd created by doing my own video and consulting no one for that first presentation. I entered the final election running against Dick Corey, a good friend and fellow straight-A student who ran on the mild-mannered "Dick-Boy Walton" theme. A painfully long Saturday brainstorming session with my family came up with five-minute skit ideas based on *Star Trek*, Mr. Rogers, the Village People, and others. But nothing appealed to me, and I petulantly asserted that we would revert to the same thing I used when I was eleven and won the Indian Hills election. We would squash Dick-Boy with "SuperRich," the powerful icon leader who could cure a mysterious pestilence, thwart evil criminals, perform flips and handsprings, and of course show himself as the best possible choice for student body president.

It was the most stressful week of my life. I'd recently been diagnosed with mononucleosis and suffered from fatigue and sore throat. I'd created significant friction in the family through disagreements and ingratitude. My opponent was working with Jane Breinholt, the neighborhood mastermind in high school elections. She was also assisting other candidates, all of whom had formed a tight-knit clique of potential winners for different offices. Ironically, I too worked with Jane, creating an awkward situation in crossing paths with a group that seemed to be running on a platform with Dick-Boy Corey. It was literally me in one room of the house and the Dick-Boy groupies in the other room. The awkwardness was a precursor of a year to come: me as president, Dick receiving the concession office of vice president over activities, and the rest of Jane's group all winners for their prospective offices.

"SuperRich" was, admittedly, a huge success. The skit featured powerful music, a simple story about people who needed a hero, and SuperRich coming to save the day. I can still feel the colossal sensation I had while standing on a wall high above an audience of two thousand high school students, belting out a primeval yell as the spotlights found me and I rushed to the stage. Jane said that at that moment, she knew I'd won the election. There was no hope for Dick after the dominating excitement that our skit had brought to the auditorium.

I'm not sure that being president of the school was my best year. As a cheerleader, I had fun with the group and got really good at gymnastics tricks with my partner, Jenny Christensen. Now I moved on to the solitary position of leadership. The school had a tradition of standing up for me when I entered the auditorium to start assemblies. I was on the intra-school TV channel almost every day. I held a permanent hall pass and a set of keys to the offices, the gym, the auditorium, and the secret basement tunnels. The other student body officers expected leadership from me, and I was weak to perform. No one had really gotten over the election setup: me in one room, the gang in the other.

I wonder if my mom and Diana knew all along that the president is a position of isolation. There were many student government offices held in our family, including class officers, historian, and vice president. But president was the pinnacle. It was a great accomplishment for me and for the family. Great accomplishments also came with regret for what was left behind. Mom said that I was achievement oriented from birth. I am constantly seeking some external goal. But I miss a lot along the way and sometimes step on others to get where I'm going. Rarely do I find true happiness when I've arrived. And when I'm there, I'm usually alone.

When the election was over, I failed to thank Diana for all she'd done. I moved on, taking my kudos and preparing for the upcoming summer. Finally, one day, about two weeks later, Mom hinted that I should perhaps offer a token of thanks to Diana, perhaps some flowers or something. Embarrassed by my slowness, I took a bouquet to her with a short note. She received it, knowing that it was not my idea. I was not that selfless. I'd reach a goal and fall into my typical "look at me" mode. It was not the type of social popularity that Diana had shown me or expected of me.

These were the memories brought on by a mountain snowstorm of that first ski trip with my big sister. I have offended Diana many times over the years. I once told her that I didn't want to be part of the "east bench dynasty" that she wanted for the Allen family and instead moved my family to my wife's rural hometown in Canada. I regret that phrase so much, especially since just a few years later, I would indeed move my family to Salt Lake City's east side and want, as she wanted, a close connection of cousins. Just like a mother, Diana was usually right in the end. I admire her and appreciate her. But to this day, I interact uncomfortably with her, perhaps fearful of disapproval, just like a seven-year-old boy once ruined a day of skiing.

The snow was gone now, just like those early memories, melted into adulthood where siblings take their separate paths and remain only loosely connected with those whom they once shared every day, every meal, and every car ride. I left the huddled group of runners at Aid Station #4, anxious to get off the pass and out of the wind. The fog had cleared, and I could see blue sky to the east. I'd taken on about three hundred calories and would begin sipping from my protein recovery drink.

Best of all, I was commencing a three-thousand-foot drop over the next five miles. I felt a great burst of freedom, leaving behind the snow, the cold, and the long morning of fog. Now I could fly. It was just like the feeling I had when Bryan and I stood, overlooking the Grand Canyon. I stood with my arms stretched out, imagining what it would be like to fly down to the

Colorado River. Like the time Dad and I stood atop King's Peak, cautiously approaching the sheer cliff face on the west side. I pictured a thousand-foot cable zip line that I would grab and buzz down, mimicking the G.I. Joe string line that I played with in the backyard. Like being on top of KenDing Mountain in southern Taiwan, looking out to the blue ocean and wanting to fly down and off the island, to escape the daily duties of a missionary and instead sail unrestrained to wherever I wanted. It was like skiing down Diamond Lane, the steep corduroy-groomed run off of the Powderhorn ski lift at Solitude. The wind pushed my parka up against my chest and arms and made it feel like I had wings that would at any moment carry me off the icy surface and let me glide down the mountain on a stream of air. Now I had that same sensation as I raced down a wide trail into my seventeenth mile and beyond.

Chapter 4: Cohleen: Sandcastles, Dirt Pies, and Silly Mud

If I have wrongfully neglected anyone in this life, it is my sister Coke. Eighteen months and two grades younger, she looked up to me for direction, advice, and, most of all, friendship. I can't think of how many times I let her down. I was never entirely cognizant of shutting her out and did not purposely disavow little sister for reasons such as my own popularity. Indeed, for a time in high school, I was proud to be known as "Coke's big brother" rather than she being known as "the president's little sister." But even if my own self-assured security was not at stake, I could not find the means to be closer to her. While I desperately sought closeness in girlfriends, I didn't want the companionship that Coke so often had to offer. Friday nights with nothing to do, and I would be in my room alone, leaving her to watch TV and hope that I'd come out to play a game.

I'm sure there was just enough pride in me that dipping down to befriend little sister was not cool. Maybe a gender difference made sibling friendships unnatural for me in the adolescent years. By age twenty, I came to realize that I was personally very unhappy, and yet still my search for happiness in girls, in school, and in life discluded the obvious relationship that was tugging at my sleeve.

I was twenty-one as we explored Manhattan together. At Mom's suggestion, we'd flown to Washington, DC, and spent a couple of days camping out in the apartment of a distant friend. Then we joined Diana and Dave and got to see our first nephew, six-month-old Michael, living in Charlottesville, Virginia. From there we took the train north to Philadelphia for the afternoon, and then arrived in the late evening at Grand Central Station in New York City, where brother Dave picked us up. He and Loke lived in a one-room apartment in upper Manhattan, where he was attending law school at Columbia. They hosted us for a few days before sending us back home again.

The trip was a brilliant success and filled with grand memories of the Blue Ridge Mountains, Thomas Jefferson's

Monticello, the National Gallery of Art, Independence Hall and the Liberty Bell, *Les Misérables* on Broadway, and New York's Chinatown. In the travel hours, Coke and I filled the time with a fifteen-game Scrabble match, which I narrowly won 8–7 as we flew over Denver on the way home. Coke has since memorized much of the Scrabble dictionary, and I cannot challenge her prowess of the game. But the memory of that great trip together remains indelible in my mind.

    The memory is not all positive. Despite the great sites and experiences and the golden chance to create a forever bond with my sister, I struggled with that friendship. It was leaving Central Park where I realized how cold I'd become. We were walking home from the Metropolitan Museum of Art, climbing the 110th Street hill as it approaches St. John's Cathedral. I remember the exact location because of all of our travels, all our time together, all the walking we'd done that day, it was leaving Central Park where she started to cry. I was the cause of her tears. I was, to be honest, tired of her. I was tired in general, which didn't help in this situation. But tired of being around her. Too much time together, I suppose, even for siblings. And in my moment of disconnectedness, I turned to the standby solution that Mom said that Dad and I shared: silence. We walked 110th Street in silence. A slow cab passed us. The fall trees rustled. The distant city clamored in a dull afternoon roar.

    It is in these moments that Coke shines. She is able, in the heart of difficulty, to express an optimistic idiom, to sing the cheerful tune of something she learned at girl's camp, or to tell the same dumb joke she has told for years so that we can laugh at it.

    "Ju-neau what the capital of Alaska is?" she broke the silence.

    I mumbled nothingness, refusing to answer "Juneau" and ruin the joke, or to answer "no" and force her to continue her wordplay on inquiries: "D-j-eat? No, d-j-you?"

    "Well, I went to Chicago, and I walked around the block …" she again started the annoying camp song that we only partially knew. Annoying to me at that moment, but in prior days we'd laughed ourselves silly trying to recall how the song ended, and then composing lyrics of our own. But I was in no mood for songs or for jokes.

One might say that we suffered the simple fate of two people, any two people, be they friends, siblings, or married partners, who've spent too much time together. Scrabble is not a short game, and the fact that we'd racked up fifteen games within a week is a sure sign of too much togetherness. We'd sat by each other in flight, slept on adjoining couches in someone's tiny apartment, and seen every painting and sculpture and famous site together. It seemed like we just needed a rest from each other. But that feeling of too much togetherness was one-sided: my sided. Coke did not and would not feel that way.

I was twenty-one, entering my third year of school and trying to make important decisions about a college major and a future career. She was a college freshman, bubbling with new independence and ready to see and do everything the world had to offer. I was lonely and forlorn, pining over a Canadian girl I'd met that year and troubled by our distance. Coke was carefree and unattached, seeking adventure over romance. And frankly, I was always the somber child. Mom had charcoal sketches done of each of the seven children, full-sized framed and still hanging in her basement. I am the somber one, meticulously piecing together a model ship at about age ten, not unhappy but noticeably unsmiling. Coke, on the other hand, stands next to tall flowers, her beautiful flowing black hair and her lovely smile capturing the essence of her eternal persona.

"The Lord said to Noah, you're gonna build an arky arky …" Songs which have since entertained my children around the campfire were at that moment the most obnoxious thing I could imagine. I ignored the attempts at frivolity and focused myself on getting us home to the apartment. She was tearful, but even as I recognized how I'd hurt her, I was unable to apologize or make amends. The hurt was not so much in that very moment, although clearly I was a poor travel companion. But it was years of neglect, caring little about the happenings of her life, focused only on my own. Big brothers can be heroes, but I was not one.

She and I used to walk together, usually Sunday evenings. We called it our "walkabout" and usually traversed the mountain road toward the painted "H" on a huge rock outcropping above our house. It was a beautiful panoramic view of the valley, and we enjoyed it in every season and weather. Then one day, I stopped walking. Elizabeth was in my life, and I spent Sunday evenings with her instead. I later discovered that Coke continued our walkabouts, but all alone, into her midtwenties.

    I was reminded of her and our walks together on an interminable dirt road canyon, which slowly climbed toward Squaw Peak mile thirty. Following a short paved section through a residential area, the dirt road followed a stream up a narrow canyon in which direction I will never know. There were no signs to name the canyon road or stream, no addresses on the homes we'd just passed, and no view of anything to help me get my bearings. I was disoriented, following the occasional orange ribbon tied to a tree marking the right course. I passed no one, and no one passed me. I saw no one for over an hour, winding my way through the aspen canyon with frequent stream crossings and no sign of human life. I ran some, and then walked a lot, chiding myself for not running the whole portion of this easy climb. I snacked on raisins and thought of dropping some, letting my mind wander to Hansel and Gretel, marking trails, and the time at age five I got separated and lost from the family at Mirror Lake. Just stay where you are, we were taught.

    From my pocket I pulled the homemade spreadsheet, which I had carefully created with mileage, estimated times, and elevation gains. The paper was wet and tore easily, and I'd made the mistake of printing on both sides, which now showed through and made the chart blurry. It was the closest thing I had to a map but now wet and blurred and almost useless. It appeared that the paved section and the dirt road canyon comprised almost eight miles together, or roughly two hours. I was about one lonely hour away from one of the greatest moments in the race: a change of shoes. I had carefully planned the change, placing my best running shoes in the drop bag for Aid Station #7 based on the approximate point just before the second major hill climb. But I'd not planned for mud and snow, and my soggy shoes and socks had distressed me most of the morning. Somewhere in the next hour, "just around the next bend," I would say a thousand times, I would get to change to dry socks and new shoes.

    The rain was gone now, the clouds parting, and the blue sky and sunshine warmed up that canyon. I felt lonely and wished for someone to walk with. Throughout the day it seemed that even when my pace had matched someone for a few minutes or half an hour, we had little to say to each other. "Knee problems?" I'd been asked more than once, inquiring about the wrap I wore around my right knee. But that was about it for conversation. I expected more. I thought that sharing a brutal fifty-mile race would bring me together with interesting people. I imagined visiting with half a dozen people for several miles each, talking and sharing our stories of how we trained, why we were on Squaw Peak, and who was waiting at the finish line. The aid stations were full of friendly volunteers offering drinks and food, congratulating us on making it that far. Welcoming, but not necessarily warm. No one to call me by name. No one to care that I had a family, that I was a doctor, that it was my first race. No one like my sister Coke.

We knew that Coke would make a good school teacher. She was so animated and fun. If I described an event to my parents, whether I liked or disliked it, I would do with my usual monotonous ennui, especially pronounced as a teenager. But Coke would tell about catching the fish with marvelous animation.

"Suddenly, the string went *zing*, and I panicked!" she said.

"You mean the line—fishing line," I corrected.

"Whatever, the clear string stuff that has a big floppy fish on one end and a scared little girl on the other!"

"What did you do?" Mom asked.

"So I grabbed my pole, and I couldn't believe it—the end was bending 'uwah wah wah.'" She held an arm high and then bent it over while making springing noises. "I thought it was going to break, so I pointed it out to where the string, er … line was going out into the water—like, duh, if the stick's bending too much, then stop the bending, right? But then Dave came over, and he said not to point it but to let it bend and help fight the fish. Me! Little me fighting a fish!"

"Oh, my goodness!" Mom loved Coke's animation, totally enthralled and entertained by a description of even the smallest of events.

"So then he told me to wind that thing and bring the fish in."

"Reel," I corrected.

"That thing that winds the string, but it was hard—there was a fightin' fish on the other end!"

"Could you see it?" Mom asked.

"Well, so I'm winding that reel, and he's fightin', and the pole is bending 'uwah wah wah,' and I can barely see with the sun right in my face, but suddenly that big mad fish jumped out of the water!" Coke's whole body told the story, reeling, pulling, jumping, staring out into the sun. She fell back to the ground.

"I fell back because suddenly the string wasn't tight, and I thought, *Oh no, I've lost him off the hook,* but it was just that he jumped. So then I was back on, winding him in, but he was getting weaker and weaker, poor little fishy with a hook in his mouth." She made the sad face of a wide-mouth bass, even though it was rainbow trout we were after.

"Was he little?" Mom asked.

"Heck no! He was a big fishy! I just say 'poor little fish' because he was probably somebody's baby fish, but he was a big jumper!"

"Twelve inches," I said.

"Hold on! Don't go telling my big fish story," she chided playfully. By now Mom was fully amused, soaking up every moment of her animated thirteen-year-old and her angling experience.

I could never be so animated, even if I really tried hard. Coke made actions and sound effects and body motions to describe things. I have a daughter, Madison, who does the same. It's not showing off or overdoing it but vivacious, energetic, taking a life experience and making the very most of it. Life is passionate, and every experience has meaning. Real tangible existential meaning. For me, it was about getting through life and getting to the end. We hiked to the top of Bald Mountain so that we could get to the end and look around, and then turn around and come back. We accomplished something. We reached the summit and could now conclude that it was done and achieved. But for Coke, the top didn't matter. It was the rock formations along the way. People stacked up those rocks, and she wondered who they were and what they were like. Ants scurried across the trail, and she'd follow them to their home, fascinated by a complex series of ant hallways and tunnels that she could only imagine but couldn't see beneath the single hole in a sandy top. It was the flowers, as in "stop and smell the flowers." But not just smell them, pick them, caress them, rub their purple petals on your cheeks, and feed them to the caterpillars. For me, the view from the top was the ultimate sign of "being there." But for Coke, the view changed every few minutes as we climbed. The view of the top was more interesting than the view from the top.

It was the same in Manhattan. As we left Central Park and trudged up 100th Street toward Columbia Law School and Dave's tiny apartment, I lapsed into silence, and Coke, after multiple attempts at being playful and fun, cried and recognized what a miserable companion I was. We'd been to the Metropolitan Museum of Art. We'd done it. We'd accomplished that part of the trip. Now I was tired and just wanted to go home and rest. But accomplishing things and ticking them off a list was not Coke's way. Central Park was more interesting. The pathways leading off to hidden gardens and monuments. The vendors and their rich smoky bratwurst, fresh-cut French fries, and giant pink cotton candy. Couples rollerblading, smiling, laughing at their awkwardness, falling on to the grass and rolling into each other. I simply followed the small map I had in the centerfold of a tourist magazine. There was a relatively clear path from the Met to the northwest corner of the enormous park. But Coke wanted to follow those unfamiliar paths.

"Let's just see what the fountain looks like," she said.

"It's just a little fountain," I responded, "and it's the wrong direction."

"Come on, what can it hurt?" It was the same tone I'd often heard Mom use. She was always trying to convince Dad to try something different or do something just a little bit off his normal routine. They discovered fresh apples in Santaquin, in the red barn a mile off the freeway. I would never have gotten off the freeway in Santaquin. When you're on the freeway and headed to St. George, you don't stop in a tiny town with no services, even if they do have apples. It's just not part of the plan—the plan is to go and get to your destination, making one necessary restroom stop in Cedar City. But not following random signs for Lavender Living Farms, Cove Fort Historic Site, and especially not apples in Santaquin.

"Maybe there's a special Chinese garden down there," Coke entreated. "Maybe the noodle man is down there with his special Taiwanese 'no row' noodles."

"Nyou rou myan?" I answered in perfect Mandarin. I'd been home from Taiwan less than three months, still traumatized but also entranced by a culture where I had spent two years. "I highly doubt there's 'nyou rou myan' down that path," I laughed, giving in to her lead.

"Come on!" She pulled me down to the fountain, where our best travel photo was taken and remains a dear treasure to me. No noodles, no special garden, nothing particularly interesting. Interesting to me, that is. Coke found everything interesting: the lofty trees, the pond, the lily pads, the old copper fountain now stained green and mossy, the solitary artist sitting on a retaining wall and sketching fish.

Coke saw things that I did not see. We'd had a three-hour stopover in Philadelphia between DC and New York. It was a mad dash for the Liberty Bell, approximately one mile from the train station. I jumped out of the train and started a brisk walk, carrying my single large backpack with all of my belongings. Coke straggled behind, three or four smaller bags and a backpack dangling from her arms. That's how I'd see her on the university campus: loaded down with textbooks, two bags, a purse, sunglasses, and an apple. You almost wanted to give her a shopping cart for all her things or at least offer to carry a bag or two for her.

"Hey Smoke!" I'd finally learned to befriend my sister on campus, which I did very little of in high school. "You need a locker!"

"It's making me strong!" she'd say. "It's called 'textbook bodybuilding 101.'"

"Really, can't you leave some home, or in the car?"

"Then I have to go back to my car, which is way over in 'E' parking, then come back to the library, then I'd forget something, and go back, and never get to studying."

"A little lunch on the go?" I said, pointing to the apple.

"D-j-eat?" she asked.

"No, d-j-you?" I fell into it every time. It was, admittedly, a funny thing we shared. I had very few funny things in my life but could share just this little funny phrase with her.

"D-j-you-know what the capital of Alaska is?" she played.

"Fairbanks?"

"Ha-ha, goofball."

"I just can't keep up with the geography major," I said, exasperated.

"Geography minor, you'll recall," she corrected. "I am going to be a school teacher."

"Yes, Miss Affleck." Our favorite second grade teacher. Her lifelong hero. She would later student teach with the beloved Miss Affleck.

In Philadelphia, we walked fast, she with her dangling bags and I with my one backpack. I knew exactly where to go and recognized the street names and direction to walk as soon as we climbed out of the train station. As if with blinders on, I started walking to the Liberty Bell.

Philadelphia is not a beautiful city, at least in my experience. Having just left beautiful Charlottesville, Virginia, with its vineyards and elm trees and green hills, we were now shockingly surrounded by decrepit brick buildings, a hodgepodge of apartments, and crowds of people. Of course, I didn't notice much of that, as I set out straight for the Liberty Bell.

Coke noticed all of it. She didn't care much for the Liberty Bell, except that it was our destination. But the path was always more interesting than the destination. She saw groups of young black kids and wondered why they were out of school midday in September. Old brick apartments with iron fire escapes and heavy laden laundry lines between buildings. Just like we'd seen on *NYPD Blue* and other eastern big city shows. Graffiti everywhere, some gray random sprays or lettering that could hardly be discerned, and other colorful bright red artistic designs and symbols. Tourists surrounded us, mostly older folks, remarkable standouts from locals who were on their way to Walgreens, ShopRite, and Gusto Pizza. Twenty or thirty people would crowd together on a street corner, waiting for the green light. Then they'd bustle into each other as they crossed the street, total strangers rubbing so close that we could smell each person as they passed: cigarette smoke, spicy sausage, alcohol, body odor. Urban kids with dyed hair, piercings, dark makeup, all-black raggy clothes. Businessmen in cheap suits on their way to a job interview or a downtown office. Tourists in tropical shirts and Bermuda shorts, their sagging tanned facial skin, their

Payless walking shoes. Blue-uniformed cops in companionships, one Mediterranean skinny, scraggly, but looking wise and seasoned, the other overweight Caucasian looking dopey and new.

We stood in line for the Liberty Bell and took the tour of Independence Hall. Now we could say we'd done it. Nothing spectacular for either of us. We stopped for a few minutes to munch "gorp," Mom's blend of peanuts, raisins, and M&M's candies. Then it was back the same way we'd come, to the train station and onward.

We didn't talk much on the train. That is perhaps when I started noticing that I was tired of having a traveling companion. I was reminded of the two years in Taiwan, living and working with a missionary companion twenty-four hours a day, every day, for two years. I learned to love my alone time. At least, most of the time I enjoyed solitude. Then I was desperate for companionship. Like Holden Caulfield in *Catcher in the Rye*, one moment seeking the companionship of others and the next trying to get away and just be alone.

Too tired to start up another Scrabble game, we mostly drifted in and out of sleep while passing through New Jersey and Delaware.

"What did 'Della wear' to the party?" Coke asked in a smiling half stupor. It seemed that even in her sleep, she was ready with a quip or to start up a game.

"Her 'new jersey,'" I replied without engaging her. I looked out the window at fog over the water. I knew the next part of the states game: washing ton, 'Minnie's soda,' and the thing the Tenne did see. But I was in no mood to play along. I closed my eyes, and neither of us spoke again until Grand Central Station.

Solitude can only go so far. Even for those of us who enjoy being alone, basking in silence or talking to ourselves, there comes a point when we need human interaction. It's like we need someone to reflect off of, to be sure we're still human and not morphing in to a state of un-being. While the sun was now high and the morning snow and darkness lifted, I found myself inextricably stuck in a narrow canyon with no view and no perspective. The gravel road went on, and I knew that eventually,

I would reach the next aid station, the next Powerade, human support, though minimal, and a change of shoes. But it was a long hour. Almost worse than fog, now rocky hills and trees in a narrow canyon blocked my view of anything. And again, I was surprised that no other runners caught up to me, and that I caught up to no one. We were just beyond 26.2 miles, the point at which a marathon becomes an ultra-marathon. This was beyond what the typical runner trains for, the ultimate distance experience for thousands of runners. In that period of loneliness, I started to feel a little crazy, my sun-warmed head dizzy with frenzied thoughts: why go on? Why was I here? What good was the accomplishment of an ultra-marathon? What does this mean about my life? Why did I hate people and love them at the same time?

I alternated short jogs with walking, playing little games in my mind about running to the next bend, and then walking around the corner. But more often than not, I couldn't run to the next bend, stopping early and chastising myself for not being able to make it that short little distance. With every bend, I hoped to turn and find a group of people to say hi to, or the aid station suddenly come up, or picnickers, or even a mountain lion. Something to break the monotony. All along knowing there was nothing for a full hour. I checked my watch every two minutes, and slowly that hour ticked by.

Coke was a marvelous gamer. Not video games, as she was young enough in the early '80s to miss the brothers' Atari fascination. Not athletics, though she too would dabble in tennis, and even run a Triathlon in her twenties. But real games, as she called them: board games and card games. Scrabble has possibly been her lifetime favorite, though I wonder now if Scrabble wasn't just a compromise for something that others would play. She knew that in my free time I would sit down for a game of Scrabble, especially if Dad played with us. Then it was like challenging the master, the man who'd red-penciled all our English essays and spent much of his life reviewing legal contracts for correct wording. Dad was slow and methodical, and I enjoyed sitting down with him on a Sunday evening.

Coke, on the other hand, was fast-moving and quick-thinking. She was ready to put her next word down without delay.

She saw spaces and word connections that I didn't see. Dad and I contemplated long words that always covered a double or triple word score and sometimes took several minutes to play our letters. Coke buzzed through with lots of small words, filling corners that would give her points in two directions. In the end, our older and wiser word prowess was rarely a match for her quickness and small word play. From a young age, my sister was embarrassingly good at games.

      Scrabble was likely a compromise because she knew I'd play it, but given her preference, she'd beat me at Uno any day, or Sorry, or checkers. Even Monopoly moved quickly with Coke; she cruised around the board and bought up properties faster than I could keep track. She liked to move quickly through a game, impatiently waiting for me to look at my cards or calculate my next move. She wanted to get through it so that we could start again, one Uno game following another and another. As an adult, she got into "fast Scrabble," using the letter tiles to individually build word patterns in a fast-paced game lasting less than ten minutes. I couldn't do it. If I'm going to play a game, I like to sit down and concentrate, feeling fulfilled by one well-played effort. But she was fast, winning one match and ready to go again. Games were life, and life was fun, continuous fun.

The exception to the fast and furious games, and perhaps the ultimate event for my game-loving sister, and perhaps the supreme dread of my entire teenage life, was the game of Risk. Risk was at least a six-hour occasion, if not twelve or more. We'd been known to have one continuous game going several days and nights during the Christmas holidays between family dinners and skiing and requisite sleep time. In fact, I've probably only played Risk two or three times in my life, convinced by Coke that we had hours of time and nothing better to do, and going so far in her begging as to concede the continent of Asia to me at the start, and probably throwing in some bribery candy or money or promising me her firstborn, just to get me to sit down and play the world's painfully longest most difficult dreaded board game: Risk. Now the fun was not in fast-moving play, beating family and friends in quick matches of Rook and Go Fish, but in a long drawn-out competitive strategy game, "taking over the world" as it were.

My smiling cute long-haired baby sister taking over the world. The symbolism was apparent to me in my midteens. She was going to succeed in life. She would succeed because "success" is finding joy in life. I would spend my years yearning for success in position, popularity, college degrees, and economic gain. But for Coke, it was just fun. As fun to play a game as to win it. For me, winning the occasional Scrabble game would confer a feeling of superiority and pride. For Coke, winning was just additional fun to playing the game. And life was a game, fun and fast-moving, finding joy in experiences along the way, and creating fun when rainy days and adversity wanted to get you down. She turned crying into laughter. She made mud pies from fallen sandcastles. Her goodness and happiness would spread over her world and those around her, just as her red figurines filled the board in our game of Risk. She would succeed in life. She too would run for student body officer and win, achieve popularity, a masters degree, missionary service in Wales, and many other accomplishments. But she did so effortlessly, laughing at her own mistakes, making a game of temporary pitfalls. Unlike big brother, stressfully working to achieve goals, finding joy neither in the hike nor in the view from the top. Our adult situations are remarkably similar in family life and socioeconomic status, and yet we're polar opposites in what we get out of life. I'm still working to get to the end of the rainbow, while she's been full of color all along.

By mile twenty-eight, this fact was agonizingly apparent to me. I was on the achievement path again, the ultra-marathon my latest attempt to accomplish something great and to be known for it. In the narrow canyon called Hobble Creek, lonely and viewless and fatigued, I thought of how Coke would turn this into adventure and fun. Of course Coke would probably not be here in the first place, because an ultra-marathon was a stupid hollow ambition with no game value to it.

Life was not any easier for Coke than anyone else, and I'd seen her in discouraging times. Coke didn't marry until her late twenties. The right man never came along. Those were some lonely and difficult years, especially in Utah where "old maid" status is ostracized by twenty-five. Coke excelled in school, obtaining an elementary teaching certificate with honors, a minor in geography, and then a masters in piano pedagogy. She traveled the world with every opportunity: study abroad in Israel, New Zealand with Mom and Dad, China with Diana, Great Britain, Peru, and other places. She camped a lot, sometimes alone or with an adventurous current boyfriend, much to the chagrin of my parents. She worked at ZCMI clothing, building an impressive wardrobe and savings account. Most of all, Coke was always in good spirits. Even when she was down, she'd laugh about discouragement. Lemonade from lemons.

Once I remember giving myself fully to her imagination and games. It was just after I'd graduated from high school when we drove to Southern Utah to hike the Narrows section of Zion National Park. Something we'd both wanted to do but never had the chance until then. We packed our backpacks for a quick one-night trip to Zions and drove Dad's blue VW Quantum. I remember thinking what a cushy ride it was, like riding on air and yet soft and squishy handling as I tried to change lanes or turn. It wasn't until Cedar City that I finally clued in that the tires were only at 12 psi instead of 35 psi. One could say it was my youth and inexperience that didn't recognize a problem with the car until four hours into the drive. But I think it represents how enthralled we were in conversation. Conversation primarily driven by Coke, sixteen, full of life, blossomed from a little girl into an engaging young woman. I was essentially on a date with my younger sister, recognizing what a great date she was.

Turning off the interstate, we headed east and noted ominous dark clouds in the distance. Horrifying tales of flash floods in the Narrows were front and center in our minds, two adventuresome but novice hikers in areas of southern Utah. We pressed on, confident that things would go well and knowing all along that we were adventurous, but not unwise. We were not big risk takers, not like Bryan, who would welcome the chance to challenge those stories and face the dangerous elements just to prove that he could. Coke and I were here for fun, not for bragging rights. If the water was muddy, or the storm clouds thick, or the canyon simply felt unsafe to us, we'd go hike Angel's Landing or Emerald Pools and enjoy our camping trip just the same. For once I was thinking like she thought, not of the destination and the accomplishment of the Narrows, but of fun along the way.

Suddenly, Coke was telling a story. Like I was a child, cozying into bed, though I was driving, she started telling a bedtime story. The words flowed like chocolate syrup as she developed an amusing imaginary tale. Like twins in a moving Volkswagen pod I was overwhelmed by a warm kinship which superseded any hint of embarrassment that an eighteen-year-old might feel in being on a camping trip with his little sister instead of his buddies.

"Once upon a time in a castle far, far away," she started.

"Story time?" I laughed. "With princes and dragons?"

"There lived an old wizard king," she continued. "The castle was not a castle at all, but a red-rock mountain fortress with forty-two rooms carved from ancient caves."

I pondered on the choice of forty-two for number of rooms in a castle, and then looked ahead and saw in the distance a domed red-rock formation atop a high bluff, bathed in morning sunlight amid the backdrop of black clouds. There was the castle. Remarkable how she could spontaneously capture a vision and weave it into a story.

"Forty-two rooms?" I queried sarcastically. "How about a dungeon?"

"The king had been banished from the land of Nakorem," she continued despite my flippancy. "His wizard powers, once used for good, eventually drew him to a group of evil sorcerers."

"What's the difference between a sorcerer and a wizard?" I asked, trying to throw off her silly story.

"His name," she paused. "His name was Ramikish!"

Where did Ramikish come from? Rachmaninoff? Rasputin? Ramekin dishes? I had to wonder how she had so suddenly chosen this unusual character name. Perhaps she'd told a similar story before, and was now improving upon it with the surrounding red rock mountains and impending storm. Or she was just gifted with imagination and fantasy and fun. I have never forgotten that name, or the story.

"There must be a *girl*," I added, "a princess locked away in the tower, maybe?"

"Yes, there is a girl," she now responded to me, recognizing that I was no longer facetious, but interested, embraced by the tale and the mountain and the storm. "When Ramikish was banished from the land of Nakorem, he kidnapped the princess daughter of the new king. Her name was Keziah."

Coke's story took us through the winding road, intensifying as we approached the rock dome which we secretly knew to be the castle of evil Ramikish. The road then climbed out of the canyon and passed through two tunnels carved through the red rock mountain. Every aspect of the terrain added to the story, sometimes humorous and other times sinister, realistic, or philosophically challenging. In all my years I would not have thought that I'd find such fulfillment and retain such memories from cruising in a car with my baby sister telling childhood fantasy stories.

The Narrows hike is disappointing from the top. It takes several hours wandering through desert ranchland before you even see red rocks and river. We were unaware of the shuttle service which allows hikers to go through the full sixteen-mile passage and meet their car parked at the bottom, and so we'd planned instead to hike in eight to ten miles and camp, returning through Chamberlain Ranch the next morning. But the lack of scenery and interest in the first few hours was discouraging. I wonder now if starting at the bottom of the Narrows and hiking up halfway was not allowed, or if we just didn't think of it.

I am a strong hiker, and relatively fast. Even loaded with a thirty-pound pack filled with food, a tent for both of us, my sleeping bag, and a change of clothes, I got on the trail and wanted to move right along. I'm a destination hiker, taking little interest except in the most scenic of overlooks or the most fascinating rock formations and trailside flowers. But otherwise I'm headed toward the destination and not wont to stop. I'm a strong hiker, but a very poor companion hiker. Visiting is not my forte. Chatting is totally foreign to me. I'm a good public speaker, but not a good private speaker. I am so like my dad: Mom does 95 percent of the talking, and he adds the occasional "yes" or "no, I don't think so," showing that he's paying attention. Coke kept up without much trouble, stopping for water more often that I wanted but never fussing with photos, finding things on the trail, or stopping to smell the wildflowers. She carried a twenty-pound pack, and I was impressed with her conditioning. She was not invited to the famous King's Peak hike a few years earlier, but now at sixteen, I'm sure she would have managed just as well as the boys.

Internally, I wrestle with my inability to be a conversationalist. I want to talk, joke, discuss things, even superficial conversation, but it just doesn't come out. As we maintained pace and started into a more narrow portion of red-rock canyon, the guilt of my poor companionship began to weigh more than my pack.

"I guess that storm went the other way," I said.

"The rain would have been nice to cool us off," she replied with some exhaustion in her voice.

"But we might not be able to be in the Narrows if it were raining," I retorted.

"I know, I know. It just sounds nice to have a little shower of rain right now. A cool mist of rain, not heavy pelting hide-in-a-cave rain, but gray mists that blow in and give everything a bit of moisture—the dust, the lizards, my face."

"This is the desert, you know," I reminded her of reality.

"Less than twenty inches of rain annually," she quoted

the climate notice that we'd seen on a map while getting our backpacking permits.

Then I knew I'd shut her down. I attempted to make light talk about the weather, but was unable to carry it and allow the conversation to go on. Coke would have taken off, allowing images of gray mists in the desert red-rock canyon lead her into another story, or fantasizing, or at the very least memories of family trips, prior rain showers, or tales of trails we've been on together. But I couldn't let that happen. For some reason I couldn't let conversation just go on freely. It had to be checked. Now I'd shut her down.

"A little rain would be nice, though," I tried to compensate. But it was too late.

Eventually we found ourselves dropping into a canyon which slowly narrowed into a gorge. At our nadir the sandstone walls were probably forty feet high, much less than half of the eventual height of the walls which define the Narrows trail. Still, we enjoyed the idea of being on this famous hike. The trail took us in and out of the water, alternating between sand banks on either side of the stream. "Stream" was indeed the word in August, and while we saw signs of high water and imagined a torrid river running through the gorge, it was for us, thankfully, just a stream.

It was about 7:00 PM when we finally decided we'd hiked about halfway. Looking ahead the next mile or so appeared very much like the previous one, and we were unlikely to reach the tallest and narrowest section of the hike before nightfall. So we stopped on a large sandbank to set up camp. We had a single tent, but it was a spacious three-man tent with comfortable room to share and not be awkwardly pressed together. We unloaded our things and then started to put dinner together.

As the experienced backpacker of the twosome, I planned our meals and carried the supplies. Coke might have chosen something more exciting, but I insisted that Dinty Moore beef stew was the backpacker's favorite. I didn't have time to go to Kirkham's and buy freeze-dried meals, nor did I want the expense of them. And it was only one night, so carrying a can of beef stew and some oatmeal for breakfast wasn't too burdensome. I heated the stew on a propane stove, and got out a couple of rolls and some cantaloupe pieces. We didn't plan on building a fire because of the lack of wood in the area, though we both missed that part of camping out, especially when it came to dessert: Oreo cookies instead of the s'mores that we love.

Coke picked through a bit of stew and tried to act pleased. Truth is she's not a meat eater, and I'm certain that she detested it. My plan for water didn't help much either. Lacking a microfilter pump, I'd brought iodine tablets to dissolve in river water and purify it. The silty water starts brown, the iodine makes it more brown, and then I add orange Tang to overwhelm the musty iodine flavor. Silty brawny iodine Tang to drink. She bought a filter for future trips.

With dinner done and cleaned up and still an hour of daylight remaining, Coke did the most uncharacteristic thing I've ever seen of her. She went to bed.

"I'm really tired," she admitted, "so I think I'll hit the hay."

"Okay," I said, shocked and uncertain. "I'll probably stay out a while, until it gets dark."

She didn't say more. No explanation as to why we weren't going to play Uno or Scrabble. No desire to hunt lizards, or find slot canyons, or build sand castles. In all my life I'd not seen her go to bed early. On the contrary, she was the late one to stay by the campfire until all the night stars had come out. If we'd gone through all the songs she learned at Brighton Camp, she'd start another round and sing them again. Even without a fire, she could just sit and talk, as if going to bed meant the end of a trip she didn't want to end. But not tonight. She simply told me she was going to bed and she went, zipped away in the tent and leaving me alone to read the Steinbeck book I wasn't terribly interested in.

Then I knew how I'd shut her right down. All her buoyancy could only rise so much against my cranky disposition. Physically exhausted from backpacking, I had also ladened her with mental exhaustion. Without an outlet and companion for fun, she simply shut down and went to bed. The scenario would be repeated several times in our young adulthood. You would think that I had the sense to learn from it, to open up, to participate in the fantasy story, to sing along. But I never quite caught on. From New York to Zions, from Glacier to Capistrano, whether the drive to Provo or the flight to China,

Coke enjoyed fun companionship, someone to echo her laugh, to repeat silly jokes, to be a child with her. And with the golden opportunity as her closest brother, I was always too serious, too detached, and too stubborn to play that role. As our youngest brother Todd grew old enough, he and Coke developed the playful companionship that I had left behind. And to this day I feel that I neglected her.

Aid Station #7 was by far the best and most welcoming of all pit stops. Coming at the end of a lonely canyon road, I was thrilled to finally arrive at the thirty-mile mark. A tall friendly twenty-something young man met me a few yards ahead of the station, looked at my race number and then said, "You're doing great, 532." He started to run toward the pile of bags at the station and yelled back, "Awesome, just awesome!" He was running to get my bag, and he brought it to me just as I arrived at the table.

"Why don't you sit down on the grass?" He pointed toward the stream. "Let me bring you some Powerade—nuts, crackers, gummy bears?"

"Crackers would be great, thanks," I said, "and some red licorice." Just talking to someone felt good, and the royal treatment helped me feel like I was back in the race again. I plopped down on the wet grass and started to peel off my muddy shoes and socks. It didn't occur to me at that moment, but would weigh heavily on my mind in the hours that followed: how is it that some people are so good, so happy, so selfless and welcoming? Like Coke, some are blessed with a disposition of happiness. Others of us are blessed to have them in our lives.

"Here you go, 532," the lanky young man said as he set down a cup of blue Powerade and a napkin full of crackers and licorice. "Let me help you with those," he said as he started to grab my shoe and unlace it. The momentary awkwardness of having a stranger help me unlace and pull off my wet muddy stinking shoes was dissipated by the fact that I was too tired to do it myself. It felt so incredibly good to be served that I felt emotion and tears well up in my tired eyes.

"Thank you," I said with whispered exhaustion in my voice, "thank you."

"I'll check on you in a minute," he returned. "Let me

know what else I can bring you." Then he ran to help another runner.

I turned my body and crab-walked toward the stream, dipping my feet in the cool water and momentarily mesmerized by the sensation of cold and clean on my hot swollen feet. Then I washed my legs where flecks of mud had caked on up to my knees. *No blisters*, I thought as I examined my feet and washed them. I was not one to blister much since I'd learned that running shoes are better that hiking boots. The last pair of blister-causing boots I'd given up was in my early twenties, and since then I'd been on a campaign to convince family and friends that boots were bad unless you were hiking through snow. My campaign was not successful, and as the doctor on a Youth Trek a few years back, I treated hundreds of cases of blistered feet from ill-fitting boots.

My self-allotted five minutes was up, though I wanted to stay and soak in cold water for an hour or so. I dried my feet with the inverted tops of my muddy socks, then had the great pleasure of slipping on a fresh dry pair of socks and a fresh dry pair of Nike cross-training trail shoes. I've never forgotten that feeling, and had I known what a miracle fresh shoes and socks would be I would have purchased more and planned for a change every ten miles.

A pack of protein recovery drink was also in the drop bag, and I poured the powder into a water bottle. Again I had avoided stomach problems so far, and I reminded myself to take in this protein slowly over the next hour or so.

"Let me get that for you." The young man was back and took the water bottle from me. "Fill it all the way up?" he asked.

"Yes, thank you." I let him take it without argument. In the meantime, I strapped on my waist belt and filled the pocket with more licorice and a couple of cookies.

"Here you go," he said. "You're doing great, 532, keep it up!"

With that I left the #7 oasis and hiked strongly up a short hill then began running again. I felt good. I was recharged. Over the hill was a wide grassy gentle climb where a dozen runners chose different paths from trails and four-wheeler roads. The trails were slick thin slippery slimy mud, like the mud football field we once created behind the church when I was a teenager. <u>Silly</u> mud, I thought to myself as I slipped and watched others slip and fall softly in grass or gushy puddles. For the first time all day I laughed, and laughed with others and even held out a hand to help one up as we made our way through the quarter-mile silly field and on to a dry gravel road again. It felt good to be with others, and laughing despite almost seven hours of trail running. I felt strong again, and would incredibly run, not walk, most of the way to 1:00 PM to meet my brother.

Chapter 5: The Cottage Farm

How my family acquired the Cottage Farm was as much an enigma to me as how we lost it, though much less significant. To an eight-year-old understanding it meant that the orange A-frame cabin on the shore of Bear Lake was no longer ours, and that something new called the "cottage farm," reminding me of Hansel and Gretel's experience, would become our getaway destination. Bear Lake was too far for frequent excursions, and too cold so late into the Spring that we really didn't visit much. The black spiders with the white-spotted bellies which made their home around the orange cabin would no longer be our neighbors, nor would the kids with loud motorcycles who wore hats made from beer cans and lived on our same dirt road. I have not been back to our A-frame, and it is likely demolished and the entire area developed into condos. I never made the drive to Bear Lake after the cottage was ours.

It was not entirely ours, but a tenth of it was, which meant that every ten weeks or roughly two months we had a week, beginning Tuesday at noon, which was entirely ours. Sometimes our weeks would come more frequently, even two weeks together, and then it might span most all of a summer or fall without a treasured visit. The other families visited then, and though I never met or saw or heard from any of their children, I knew them by their games left out, and clothes left in the lost and found, and bikes locked in the shed. On rare occasion their family cupboard was even left open, and we would casually glance into their stock of canned goods, marshmallows, old clothes, bedsheets, and board games. But for a week at a time, the secluded farm was completely ours.

The "cottage farm" was aptly named by the locals in Midway, Utah. Our first visit was short one, an hour of acquaintance and exploration, but lived up to every fairy tale thought I may have had. She was surrounded on every side by a three-foot fence of jagged lava rock, the appearance and texture of hard coral which would give many cuts and stings to my flesh brushing by. The first floor of the house was also lava, an obvious natural resource underneath the rich soil of the surrounding valley. It was covered, however, with vines of grape and ivy and black-green moss which softened it to the touch. It was truly an old English cottage, though I had never before seen one. The stucco around the porch was like pink frosting smeared liberally over walls and pillars, and the second-floor windows were in gable design just like photos of old cottages I had seen. None of these features, however, were at all noticeable upon first glance. Not in comparison to the roof. The roof was the bright silver-frosted roof of a gingerbread house, curved at each peak and corner. It was painted silver, like mercury or new stove pipes. There were no points or edges, but it was rather molded on the house like thick silver frosting. Just like frosting.

    I don't remember how we first acquainted ourselves with the place, and the chronology of events is elusive. Over the years every spot of the home and barns and surrounding hundred acres touched my memory in sight, smell, and feel. The sight of early morning fog hanging over the river at the edge of the fields, the smell of fresh-cut hay, the feel of sharp lava rock on my hands. I remember seeing it for the first time, and then knowing it intimately, its every detail. I remember experiences by how old I was at the time, picturing myself at ten, twelve, or eighteen in a setting at the farm. Each a different season of life, and more literally a different season of the year. In some way the seasons were particularly vivid there. Perhaps it was because they had changed each time we visited, and yet we never actually saw them change. On one visit the grass was green and flourishing, and the next time we spent a week there it was brown and dead. Once snow and ice, and then water and sun, and a week not enough time to see the transition.

    We were the unwelcome city folk in Midway, Utah, the children of an attorney and growing up in the relatively large metropolis just an hour away. Our habitation of rural land seemed almost an offense to the locals, hence adding to our seclusion and solitude. We played golf there as only city kids do, rode motorcycles in the area, and even built a tennis court on what was otherwise half of an acre of good farmland. I never once met any of the neighbors, did not play with the other children from the nearby church we visited, and in fact never saw the famous local artist whose paintings have stayed in my family these many years.

The inside of the cottage was not fancy or ostentatious in any way, and showed its age in carpeting and fixtures. The spiral climbing stairway and the arched windows reminded us of the castle-like appearance of the outside, but otherwise the white stucco walls and old green carpet were entirely unimpressive. Two bedrooms upstairs were always designated as the kids' rooms, and were certainly well worn over the years. The master bedroom was bright and decorated with wicker furniture. It was just off the dining room which was in turn connected to the kitchen, allowing for very little indoor privacy. The basement was a small concrete cellar which smelled of mice and remained damp and cold year round. Unforgettable to all who came, however, was the large indoor balcony which overlooked the living room. In addition to its safety banister the balcony held a thick rope stretched between walls. It was like the deck of a ship, and while I have never heard the real story of "J.B.," whose initials ornament the front gate, we assume that he was a mariner. A pirate, perhaps. Besides this unique balcony, the home itself was not unique, or was purely functional. It was a place for gatherings, or a means of solitary escape, and placed us in the most beautiful and peaceful of surroundings.

They said that our land consisted of a hundred acres, from the cottage itself and stretching all the way back to the Provo River. In truth it didn't really matter what land was ours as it was all leased out for the neighboring farmers to use. Strangely, in all the years I spent in those fields I don't recall ever seeing neighbors or farmers, and we were never quite sure if and when we were trespassing on someone else's land or simply crossing our own. The need to be secretive added to the fantasy of the place, and as young kids we imagined ourselves sneaking around like spies to avoid confrontation with some unseen enemy.

The land itself was awesome. In early summer the irrigation ditches flowed freely and flooded out through the tall grass and hay. Barbed-wire fences separated the pastures and cattle from the tall crops, and we were warned to close any gates that we opened lest the cows find their way out. Narrow and deep-rutted dirt roads led from the cottage back to the river, a distance of about a mile and best done on foot unless you carried a spare tire on your bicycle. The silence of being far away from town and entirely secluded was like nothing I had ever experienced, and perhaps is the fondest memory of all. Sometimes I was alone, or with a friend from home, or with my brothers. Just a few kids and wide open spaces and some cows.

    The Provo River ran high in springtime and flooded over its rocky banks. It wasn't until midsummer that we would find a good slow-moving hole and brave the cool water in bare skin. Occasionally we had fishing gear and would bait our hooks with "rock crawlers" found under the smooth stones. Dave would one day become a great angler, and found his early start on the Provo. But I caught only snags on the bushy banks, and found more interest in chasing garter snakes. No week at the cottage was complete without at least one trip down to the river. Even in late fall and winter we would observe from the upstairs window of the home a hanging mist above the distant trees, and we were again drawn to the then small stream that represented the far end of our land.

    Even more popular for the hundreds of guests that we introduced to Heber Valley over the years were the "hot pots." The famous Homestead Resort had monopolized the naturally heated springs and used them for their pools, but hidden away just a short distance from the resort was an undiscovered group of volcanic pools. At least I thought they were undiscovered, wondering in my early years how beer bottles and lighters got trashed there. The water flowed from under the rocks and filled an old bathtub that was junked there, and then overflowed into the surrounding small pool. It was crystal clear and extremely hot—about 115 degrees. Yet very slowly we could ease our bodies into it. In the frigid cold of winter the contrast of hot water and cold air was potentially dangerous. But all the more exciting in youth, and the unique experience of having icicles on your hair while soaking from the neck down in boiling sulfuric water was an experience not soon forgotten. Over the years, two separate fences blocked entrance to the hot pots, and the local sheriff would regularly patrol the area. Still we found a chance to dip during every trip there: late at night in total darkness, the car parked down the highway, and a hole in the fence through the deep black mud near where the pool flowed out.

    Up the road from the hot pots was and still is the finest golf course in all of Utah: Wasatch Mountain. There were three nine-hole courses, aptly named Mountain, Lake, and Canyon. There was a time when Mike Zackrison and I had the energy and the time to play all three courses in a day. More commonly, my brother Chris and I would play nine holes together on the Mountain course. Mike and I were easily distracted chasing gophers and hunting through the trees for lost balls. One time I caught several tiny frogs in the small ponds and took them back to the cottage in my bag. The frogs escaped in the next day, and unlikely found a suitable home on the farm. Despite my not being an animal lover, I've always carried some guilt about the lost frogs.

Playing golf with Chris was different: it was all about golf. No frogs, no ball hunting, no crazy driving a golf cart. Just golf, and talking, and soaking up the mountain air. The weekdays were not crowded, and we could go out as a twosome and walk the course. We would often play two or three balls each, using the opportunity to practice difficult shots and improve our game. Chris was a skilled professional in the making, and I cherished the opportunity to be with him.

The town of Midway, Utah hardly lived up to its name, but that was exactly its appeal. Even the locals didn't seem to want to expand or grow in any way, and they readily opposed the condominium developments near the Homestead Resort. It was a quiet town where we could ride bicycles down the main street and go entirely unnoticed. We visited the penny candy store every couple of days, and the gas station next door to fill up a gallon jug for our little Yamaha 80. Occasionally we'd visit the tiny Coleman's general store for supplies, but it seemed that we never met anyone. We never caused trouble or made ourselves known. We rode past City Hall and the few shops and the remnants of decorations left over from "Swiss Days." We hiked the trail to the top of Memorial Hill for a view of the valley and to watch the gliders fly above. We occasionally visited the Homestead, but only rarely wanted to pay the money to go inside and swim. We walked around the ponds at the fish hatchery and dreamed of catching fish that big. Once we even stopped at the school playground, but again there was nobody else there. I remember everything about the town being quiet, closed up, and still.

It was a desolate and cold winter there on a stay during the early years. It might have been our first, for I was still exploring more than I subsequently needed to. Our first, and one of our last, as we discovered the hostile midwinter conditions of the mountainous area. I donned heavy moon boots and my entire ski outfit just to go outside for a few minutes, and could barely open the door with my stiff coat and mittens I stepped out on the back porch and shut the door behind me.

  I was alone and stood for a couple of minutes on the driveway, becoming aware of a very frightening nothing. It was a stillness that I could not recall feeling. No movement, nor sound. There was not the faint water drip that usually taps out on the rain gutters, nor the movement of blowing snow or birds flying south. The birds had wisely flown long before this week. There was not even the faint rumble of cars and city noises, nor the occasional murmur of a jet plane. I put my heavy mittens up to my ears as if to open them, and knew then what it was like to have once heard and then gone completely deaf.

  It was as bleak a day as I had ever seen, and everything around, even the silver roof, was gray. I slowly moved through the snow toward the adjacent house, knowing that my every squeaking footstep was disturbing the silent grazing of distant cows.

  The two-story "maid's house" was behind the cottage, and the caretakers of the cottage farm took residence in the lower level. It was a small place and housed different families through the years. I did not see them often, though they were the only other people within half a mile. I recall my mom making friends with one or two of the families, especially the women with small children. They cared for the grounds, shoveled the few cement walks, and did some cleaning on Tuesdays in between the visiting families. The second floor was ours, what we would later convert into an indoor recreation hall filled with ping pong and foosball.

  The wooden steps to the second level were covered with snow and ice and paint chips which easily peeled from its railing. I kicked some snow off of the first step and assured myself of its stability, and then slowly made my way to the top. A large wooden door was closed but not bolted, and through a small window I looked inside. Glass fragments covered the floor, and a rickety shutter was left swinging in one of the larger windows. Faded wallpaper hung one or two feet off the wall in one corner, just above a small coal burning stove. I entered the room and the sound of my boots echoed through its emptiness. I was glad to hear no mice or bats or stray cats moving about. Webs strung down from ceiling to window pane, and a thick layer of dead houseflies covered the pane itself. But nothing was crawling or buzzing or alive in that bare upper room.

    The cottage looked different from behind and above as I now viewed it through the blurred glass of those windows. Almost a haunted look, though I had never before felt anything but safety underneath its silver roof. White fields in all directions but for a single brown trail where the cows had recently headed toward a neighboring barn. Toward the back of the "game room," as we would later call it, was an old apartment with a bed frame and box springs still there. A bathroom was off to one side, the plumbing for a toilet capped up and suspended from one wall and an old sink covered heavy with dust. Just below the back room was the manager's entrance and a tool shed, and again white-covered fields with a view to the distant river.

    In my early teens, a stark contrast would come to that bare and lifeless room. I was not involved in the cleaning, but I remember the shock of seeing that same dirty upper room cleaned up and full of life with Diana's friends. The broken glass was gone, the dead flies vacuumed up, the wallpaper trimmed and repaired. Even the sink worked, and the toilet, and new lights that turned on with dangling string switches now blazed light into the once dark and dusty space. Small and plain as it was, the game room was the most exciting party house I've ever seen, bustling with young college friends that Diana entertained at the farm. They clamored over ping pong, playing a faster and more competitive game than I'd seen before. They played foosball with their whole bodies jumping around and shaking the table. Boys eight to ten years my senior with long hair and muscled enthusiasm. Pretty and playful women, some who once babysat me, flirtatious and laughing and exuberant. Groups gathered in the back room where the old mattress once stood and talked about football and college and politics. Couples held hands and talked close to one another's faces. Music played from Diana's cassette player. The many personalities of shy, extrovert, clown, loud, and intellectual were easy for me to see, even with the few seconds I was allowed into the room to deliver candy, popcorn, and root beer. Once frigid cold and decidedly messy, the game room was forever changed by my social sister into a warm and active place of entertainment.

In the spring, Coke and I took to exploring the barns and yards. Nearest the cottage itself was a two-story structure which was something between a barn and tiny house. The rock walls and window panes made it appear more the latter, but inside were dirt floors and heavy wooden doors to suggest the other. The first floor was partly underground, making the single room feel like a damp cellar. It would one day be filled to overflowing with wood scraps from the roof remodel. But in the first few years it simply remained an unusable basement room. The upper room had a wooden floor and brick walls.

"I bet the maids lived here," Coke said excitedly.

"The maids lived in the caretaker's house," I corrected.

"Well somebody lived here," she said, "maybe the pioneers."

"There we no pioneers here," I said, "it's not that old. Besides, this was probably a tool shed or a storage room." A hole in the rock wall suggested otherwise, the size and location of a stove pipe which probably exited there. A beam of light streamed through the opening.

"Well anyway, it will be our little house." Coke grabbed a broom by the door and started sweeping. I was nervous. This was no playhouse to me. There was something worrisome about it: the rock walls, mouse droppings on the wood floor, and no electricity. I was surprised at Coke's sudden ease with this strange room.

It was then that our eyes adjusted and the light filled the room just enough to see the most ominous thing about the entire Cottage Farm. In that second-story room was a human-sized gunny sack dangling precipitously from the rafters by a thin rope. It terrified me, as if we'd stumbled on to the site of a recent hanging.

"What is it?" Coke gasped with interest as we both stepped back to the doorway.

"It's a gunny sack," I stated, as if Sherlock Holmes had found the killer with a knife in him. We both stared upward for a few moments, looking for movement.

"It's a sack o' flour," she then said with ease. I could not have been more shocked. My baby sister and I had just stumbled on to the possible site of a hanging. A dead body might be in that sack. I looked for signs of blood dripping to the floor. I thought that the executioner might still be there, hiding in the shadows. I feared for our lives in this new place, now inaptly named "cottage." No wonder it was sold, as all the locals probably knew the real haunting stories of this awful place.

Instead, Coke poked at it with her broomstick.

"It's a sack o' flour," she mused. "They probably stored their flour up there so the rats wouldn't get it." Sure enough, the sack was light and swung easily when she prodded it. No dead body in there. Just a sack full of other sacks.

"Rats?" I questioned. "You think there might be rats, but you're poking it with a stick?" I put a hand on her broom to stop her. How could this eight-year-old have such little fear? Was it all just fun and games for her? I was supposed to be the brave big brother, and I was terrified at that moment. I was confused by Coke's indifference.

"Not rats now," she replied as if I were stupid, "in the pioneer times! Maybe they had to rush to leave and they left their flour sack hanging up there." She continued poking at the sack, now swinging back and forth from the rafters.

My fear of that portentous hanging sack never left me, and for whatever reason the sack remained suspended there for all the years we played at the farm. But my anxiety but was greatly assuaged when Coke indeed turned that little upper room into a playhouse. A small white-metal cupboard was moved in and became our fridge and stove. She swept the floor clean and put a cradle and doll to sleep in one corner. Occasionally we would eat a picnic lunch on a quilt laid on the floor of that cold room. When Todd was old enough I remember playing with his circus train on the wooden planks.

The rock playhouse exited to a large gravel corral which had probably not seen horses for many decades. It was instead for city kids a place to skid bikes and "do doughnuts" on motorcycles. A couple of old campers and boats were stored in the corral. A large fire pit took up one corner, surrounded by rough hewn log benches. In my early teens on clear summer evenings I sat around a bonfire listening intently to Chris's college friends.

John played the guitar and sang like John Denver, *I am*

the eagle, I live in high country, in rocky cathedrals that reach to the sky. This beautiful song was followed by a crude ditty about a man sleeping with his brother's wife. John was a graduate student in nuclear physics, a true rocket scientist. He had scraggly long hair and a big unshaven face. My picture of scientists and researchers as quiet well-kept geeky men in white lab coats was shattered by this boisterous young singer. Mom was nervous to have me sit out there with Chris's liberal friends, the graduate student crowd whose language was unguarded and jokes always immoral. But of course I relished the opportunity to be among the older kids.

Chris's friends were markedly different from Diana's. Hers were conservative college kids from well-to-do families, still wearing the high school sweaters. They too were playful and loud and full of energy, but innocent like the TV kids from the fifties I'd seen on *Happy Days*. Chris's friends were philosophers and musicians, out-of-state young freethinkers that I pictured at Woodstock, wherever that was. Some even smoked and drank beer, something entirely foreign to me and of course disallowed at our farm and home. Sitting around the campfire together the talk was less of philosophy and more of lighthearted fun and frivolity. I watched them with great interest, wondering how the other side of the world interacted. I knew nothing but bad about drinkers, smokers, open-minded college students. But sitting with them, singing with them, eating s'mores with them, they were very likeable, perhaps even more likeable than Diana's friends. They were like Chris, sensitive, likeable, and a friend to all.

I couldn't believe how alive they were: advanced students in college subjects I knew nothing about, full of conversation, singing and laughing, nothing shy or reserved about them. John, in fact, was so unreserved that he stripped naked unashamedly to dip in the hot pots late that night. The problem, besides being stark naked in front of everyone including my little sister, was that the hot pots were too hot to go in quickly and cover your privates under water. John put one foot in, and then yanked it out as if it were burned.

"Youch! You didn't tell me it was molten magma!" John complained. He stood in the faint starlight with no fig-leaf position or other attempt to cover up.

"Sorry, John," Chris answered, "they are the hot pots."

"My God! Fuzz, can you really dip in that lava bath?"

Chris looked around a moment and saw that everyone was now hesitant to enter the famous hot springs. Coke and I froze, our feet wriggling in the slimy mud as we wondered whether to abandon this expedition or proceed as normal.

"Itchie can go first," Chris said, nodding my direction.

"You're going to boil your little brother in this broth, eh?" John mused. "Let's see Itchie dive in the volcano."

With all eyes on me now I dropped my towel and shirt on a low-lying bush and walked gingerly over a sharp gravel path that led to the pool. John had to step aside to let me approach the steaming pool. I had done it dozens of times before, but suddenly I was nervous that the water was more superheated than usual. Chris's confidence in me was reassuring, to say the least. It was magnanimous in front of his college buddies to suggest that I could do something that they couldn't. I'd gone from lowly little tag-along sitting by the bonfire to the center of attention at the sulfuric pools. I thought I heard the girls snickering behind me, and hoped they were laughing at John's exposed manhood rather than my thin pre-pubescent body.

"Nice and slow," Chris urged as my first foot entered the water. "Cold air, hot water." He was reminding me of the "channeling" trick we learned in winter. The contrast of cold air and hot water was too extreme for the body, but if you could channel the cold skin into your feet and legs it felt as if you were cooling the water as you entered it.

I was in to my knees and cautiously walking on slimy moss that covered the bottom. The feet were hardest to go in to the scalding water, and then much easier from ankle to groin, and the groin the hardest of all to dip below the surface. All was silent until my swimsuit went under, and then the applause erupted.

"Looks like Itchie is a firewalker," John was impressed. The girls clapped and shouted behind him, and I turned to see Chris flashing a big smile to me. "It will be my pleasure to boil my butt with you, young sir." John again entered the water, this time quickly going in and hiding his nakedness.

Later that night, with piqued curiosity about adults and sexuality, I took the terrifying opportunity to experience my first-ever peeping on Chris's girlfriends. I sneaked outside and planted myself by the Master bathroom window as the college girls were changing out of their swimsuits and preparing to drive home. I hid in the shadows and carefully watched the back patio and listened to the gravel drive. All quiet, allowing me the unfettered view of the bathroom. The sight of a young nude woman only a few feet in front of me was stunning, almost appalling in my innocence, yet naturally enticing. It was a fitting closure to an evening spent with Chris's friends. Mom was right to be nervous.

In the thick grass and weeds bordering the hangman's room, just off the gravel corral, was a large metal swing set—the kind only seen at parks—and a sand pile in front. That's where I picture Todd, zooming Matchbox cars through a trail in the sand or swinging playfully on the horse swing. Todd and play are synonymous. At least that's how I always saw him. He played house with Coke more often than I was willing to. They built forts together out of wood scraps, old bricks, and barn blankets. Old toys were scattered all over the property, some our own and others lost by the other families. Sandcastles, sand buildings, sand pies. Trees and fences to climb, streams to ford, and buildings to explore. If the farm was fun open playland for me, it was ten times so for Todd.

The basketball court was closer to the house, and garage between. No less than a hundred barbecues and family reunions were held behind the house in that open space. When the tennis court was built we played more tennis on the basketball court than we did basketball, and a net-height stripe still exists across the back of the garage. The tennis court was fairly well hidden, but still somewhat of an eyesore when seen with the surrounding farmland. It was yet another representation of what separated the cottage farm owners from our neighbors. It was not taken good care of, and became unusable for tennis in a few years.

Opposite the fire pit in the corral at the farm was a half-open outbuilding that became the junk yard of the cottage farm. Logs, scrap wood, broken bikes and motorcycles, and irreparable boats made their way into the barn. We must have known there were rodents or spiders in there, and not once did we play games or make forts or play house in that particular space. The adjacent structures looked like three old guest houses, perhaps for the ranch hands if there were any. They were now converted to three storage rooms with padlocks on the doors. They were dilapidated and unsightly, and what remained of the glass in boarded-up windows was shot out with our b-b guns within the first of our visits. I would say that Bryan did the shooting, though I'm sure I did my share. The open rooms were dirty and bare of furniture, the largest of which now filled with usable but old bicycles and motorcycles, chained together in family groups. Our own bikes were those we had grown out of or retired from regular use: the yellow and green ten-speeds that Diana and Chris used to ride, various children's bikes painted according the last gender of child that rode them, an antique blue bike that must have come from a garage sale, and a large green tandem bike. Bikes were life-saving at the Cottage Farm: a means to the penny candy store, the river, the hot pots, or just to be out among the fields and the clean air and the quiet valley.

The tiny Yamaha 80 "minibike" with its big yellow gas tank was perhaps our most prized possession of recreation equipment. When Dad first rode the new bike into the backyard at the Wasatch house my early teen brothers were in total shock. It was so out of character that Dad had bought it, and then to see him riding the little thing and wearing a big yellow bubble helmet. For the next fifteen years, the little off-road motorcycle would become the joy of the oldest four boys. But riding a minibike in the city was limited to distant unimproved edges of the golf course where the Jeep-man wouldn't catch you. On the other hand, the farm was ideal for our toy. And Bryan showed me how to take full advantage of it.

Bryan is forever captured on the minibike in his charcoal painting, the one of each child that hangs as an heirloom in my parents' home. He is sitting on the bike with disheveled hair and an old sweatshirt, smiling rebelliously at the camera, caught at fourteen in a dreamworld of mud, motorcycles, and freedom. Summer and winter he would ride, skidding circles throughout the corral, tearing off loudly down the dirt road to the river, kicking up mud in the wet newly planted fields. He was often good enough to lug me around on the back, but a passenger is neither fun for the driver nor for the terrified rider. Most often I would just watch while he showed me how it was done: the clutch, the gearshift, the pedal brakes.

As children of a lawyer, we had limited exposure to engines and mechanics. The minibike was not just a fun plaything, but also where I first learned about pistons, carburetors, and fuel lines. By the time it was passed to me, the bike was broken more often than not. I spent hours crouched down in the garage with greasy hands removing engine parts and trying to figure out which to replace. An older rowdy neighbor boy named Mark Norris was my mentor, seeming to know all there was to know about motors small and large. But Mark had an evil spiteful side to him. He laughed a wicked laugh when our bike broke down. He constantly insulted our little bike, comparing it as a midget to the couple of motorcycles in his own garage. His language and demeanor were a bad influence on me, and Mom knew it and frequently asked me to stay away from Mark.

On the other hand, Bryan was a patient mentor. He taught me how to ride when I was barely ten. The handlebars were so wide compared to my BMX bike, and I felt unstable and feared that I would run into the barn. More than once, I panicked and dumped the bike down to the gravel, nearly smashing myself under it. But Bryan was there, taking time from his routs through the fields to let me ride. At first he sat behind me, our hands together on the clutch and throttle. The gearshift was "one down, three up" with the left foot, always confusing to me how and why neutral was somehow in between first and second gears. Gentle use of the front brake, mostly pushing the back. Using the choke on cold days, turning off the fuel line when we were done, checking the tires each time.

At ten I rode round and round the corral, staying in first gear in that enclosed space for fear that I would run through a fence. Gradually it was second gear, down the dirt road to the end of the meadow and back. I was never as daring as Bryan, but by twelve I could circle doughnuts in the corral and splash some mud in the fields. By fourteen I was illegally using the off-road bike to run to the store, to the hot pots, or the golf course. Two of us with golf bags hanging from our shoulders balanced on a little Yamaha 80 riding to the course and watching out for the sheriff at every turn.

By fifteen the minibike was gone, left in the repair shop with expenses more than the bike was worth, and we never saw it again. Bryan moved on to other interests like football and girls and windsurfing. His friends were not in to motorcycles, and in fact one of them sold me his Yamaha 125 for a mere $150. It needed some minor repairs, but nothing Mark and I couldn't fix up, and I was thrilled to have another and larger bike to use. Contrary to Bryan's friends, all of my friends had bikes, some very large and powerful dirt bikes. We became loud gang-like terror of the east-side neighborhoods. But caught by the police one too many times, my 125 was permanently relinquished to the farm for use. Within a year, when I could actually ride it legally, the bike withered away in the dust and cold winters of the old shed. I last saw it chained there to our green tandem bicycle, and for all I know it remains there.

    I'm not sure what reminded me of the Cottage Farm. I was running up Squaw Peak, past the field of silly mud, on to a new canyon road. There were no motorcycles, no golf courses, no hot pots. I was surrounded by runners now, a curious phenomenon that I would be alone for over an hour and then bunched together for the next. Perhaps it was just a happy moment that took me back to happy times, the great cabin getaway that brought all of my family together. It is memorialized as my greatest childhood memory.

Chapter 6: Bunny Was Always There

Bunny was always there. He was present every moment of my life, from my birth until just after my seventeenth birthday when he left home. Like twins, we share the frame in every Kodak moment and eight-millimeter home movie. As a toddler, I'm seen jumping up and down in the white crib, gleeful and laughing. He reaches his hand in to tickle me, and I bounced as high as the dolphin mobile hanging from the ceiling. The white crib with the lambs painted on it went to baby Cohleen two years later. Bunny and I moved to a converted closet the basement, where we would remain together in old brown bunk beds for the rest of our youth.

The story of his nickname is remarkably unclear. It is rumored that when "sponge" was a favorite putdown, Dave once yelled "spongy" down the street to a friend. Andy Brewer heard it as "Bunny," and couldn't stop laughing at Dave's little brother. No one can say whether this definitely occurred or whether it was pieced together some time later. Unfortunately for Bryan Thomas Allen, "Bunny" would stay forever. It was said that some of the Yale Law School professors even called him Bunny. I have been unable to call him anything else. It turned out to be a catchy nickname for high school election skits, and the symbol of bunny ears easily took him to Student Body Vice President.

"Dad, I'm going skiing with Bunny," Matt Davidson once told his dad.

"Ooh la la—who's this new girl?" his dad responded. For a moment Matt didn't make the connection. Bunny was no girl, despite his history of Halloween cross-dressing as a Pep Club cheerleader and as Pocahontas. In fact Bunny was all football and masculine, more than any of my brothers. He was and is very athletic, with a focus on sports and exercise dominating his life. Matt had to wonder if his dad had heard incorrectly—did he think he said "ski bunny?" Then it dawned on him. My macho brother carried a girly nickname. He and his nickname were so dissimilar that it never really occurred to us what an outsider might think if he didn't know Bunny.

There he was at mile thirty-three, as I knew he would be. The two-mile descent to the largest aid station gave me ample time to think about him. This was the great moment of the race, of his race that I was running. To meet up with him. To see him there in his expensive running gear: Nike tights and nylon shirt, Marmot jacket, Oakley sunglasses. To hear him say "hey dude" as he always did, secretly knowing that deep down inside he wanted to hug me and tell me he loved me and that he was proud of me. Just like the time when, in front of his best friends Johnny, Stayner, and Matt, he said "you're pretty funny, little brother," in response to something I'd said. Then he let me join them five-card stud and threw in my penny ante. Like the time he told John Corbett that I was the best skier in our family. Like the day we met up and shared beef noodles in Taiwan, and he told me how well I spoke Chinese. Those were some of the greatest moments in my life. The praise and kudos from others was always a boon to my self-worth, but from my next-oldest brother it was a godsend. It was the crème-de-la-crème, the ultimate feeling—stronger than Mom's kisses, stronger than Dad's "proud of you, son." It was like being accepted and befriended by the local gang leader, and although rare and temporary, those moments when Bunny took me in or said something nice about me are vivid memories.

    I don't know how he got to mile thirty-three, but I knew he'd be there. I optimistically estimated 1:00 PM for me, and I came running in right on time. He had driven his Nissan sedan through the back roads of Heber Valley that are still foreign to me, crossing the mud and streams which the race director specifically warned family and friends to avoid without a good driver and a strong four-by-four. He was handing out Red Bull when I came in, my black-and-white cow bandana partially disguising my head. "Hey dude," he said, "good to see you." That was it, but enough. No hugs or praise or "wow" from him. Just his usual casual greeting. But it was enough for me. That moment made my race entirely. It was enough that I knew he had full confidence in me, that I was strong and would make it and that he was proud of me.

    I forced myself to have some pretzels and a swallow of protein drink.

    "Do you want to stop for a while?" he asked, expecting that I would decline. I was pumped now, hardly hiding a smile at seeing my brother and ready to climb the next few miles with him.

"I'm ready," I said, "let's do this." I tried to speak his vernacular, to sound young and hip like he always did. It didn't fit me as well. I was more serious minded, more straight-laced, more pensive. And frankly, Mom said I was always more mature than Bryan. I could talk with and be friends with girls in those teen years. At seventeen he'd punch a girl on the shoulder "you're it" and play tag like a first grader. At least, that's what Mom said. Maybe deep inside he and I were more alike. But he was expressive, energetic, physical. I was meek and reflective. And spiritual. My spirituality and his blatant disbelief would become one of my parents' greatest struggles.

"Let's do this," I said. With that we left the crowded aid station behind and headed directly north into the woods. We would be alone but together for the next two hours. The thirty-three-mile station was the official "medical check point" and required runners to leave by 2:30 PM. Anyone arriving past that time was forced to drop out and be shuttled back to Vivian Park. The cutoff was primarily logistical—another seventeen miles meant certain darkness and potential danger by the final stretch. There was supposed to be a "medical check" with weight and dehydration status, but it was not enforced. It was certainly a separation point. The faster runners came and left long before the cutoff time, and the slower ones laid down, rubbed camphor on their aching feet, ate too much, and settled in for as long as they could before heading off at 2:30 PM. Thirty-three is where Bunny made his mistakes last year. Recognizing his energy depletion, he downed energy bars, recovery drink, and even a bit of lasagna for a sudden seven-hundred-calorie burst. Then he paid for it over the next three hours, stopping for thirty minutes at a time with cramps and vomiting. "A little bit, but constantly," was his advice for me. "Take in a hundred calories every thirty minutes, not a thousand all at once."

This was the most beautiful part of the day. The sun was out, the temperature perfect, and the trail through Little Valley wound back and forth through forests and small streams. The lupine wildflowers were moist and bright, a huge contrast to the fog and snow which started the day. The climb was gentle, and the conversation rewarding. The trail was rich brown earth, solid but soft, no puddles, no rocks, no slicks.

"Quite the mud day," I said.

"Funny," he said, "totally opposite of my race." Funny was his word. Odd, interesting, crazy, shocking, or incredible, it was all funny. For a well-educated man with a huge vocabulary, Bunny informally used only a few words. And he said it with a little lilt in his voice, like "isn't life ironic?"

"Last year, I almost choked on the dust in Rock Canyon," he said, elucidating the thing that was funny. "We were shedding jackets before the Hope junction,"

"It was a slippery mess this morning," I said, still not really certain which parts of the trail he was referring to. I had studied the map to a small degree, but he knew every bit of it.

"Yeah, they'll probably come in at about eight and a half," he said, and I knew he was referring to the fastest runners. "You're doin' great—keeping up your time." I think he said this to reassure me that I didn't have to be part of that fastest group. I was okay. And I was on target to beat his time, if luck would keep my guts intact and my legs strong. I was okay. There was that feeling again: approval, validation, love. Perhaps nothing drove me as strongly as that very feeling, in the race and in life. It was not a good thing to need so much validation for strength and happiness, but there it was. At that moment I knew without a doubt I would finish the race. I was on my way. And equally important, I had succeeded in my brother's eyes. Seventeen miles to go, and the most difficult hill climb at mile forty. But I knew without a doubt that I was going to finish this race which I had started almost a year earlier.

Boy Scout Kangaroo Kourt is a cruel thing to an eleven-year-old. I was the youngest at camp, not even officially a scout before age twelve. Scoutmaster Doc Knowlton let a couple of us go early to the annual Lake Powell camp. The "court" was held on the final night, and presided over by the Senior Patrol Leader. Doc was loosely involved, and allowed punishments as long as they weren't terribly dangerous or out of line. One boy was appropriately punished for his cruelty to animals by having to build a lizard home, complete with food and shelter. Someone had to strip naked, and then paddle the canoe out to the diving rocks and jump into the water. It always brought a good laugh among scouts, and the majority of court sentences seemed to carry some form of nakedness or urination. I suspect that at that age of curiosity it's nice to be reassured that the other boys also have the beginnings of pubic hair.

My punishment was cruel and intolerable, at least to me and to fellow eleven-year-old Dallin Poulsen. As the youngest, I was required to wear a diaper all during the next morning clean up. The makeshift diaper was a large trash bag wrapped between my legs and duct taped above my waist. It was not humorous to me, though everyone including Doc got a kick out of the idea. In retrospect, it was creative and appropriately allocated. But at age eleven, it was more than I could handle. I moped and complained all the rest of the evening, and then pretended not to remember at breakfast the next morning. Brian Knowlton, the rowdy son of Doc, was the first to call me on it. I sheepishly fetched the diaper and put it on, barely holding back tears as we cleaned up our campsite.

Bunny was apart from me most of the morning, not really noticing my situation. He hung out with his friends as we packed the boats for the forty-minute return trip to Doc's Ford station wagon. Then he saw me very unhappy and even close to crying, and his desire to stay cool with his friends was dominated something else. He came to me and made an end of it.

"You're done," he said. I ripped off the diaper without saying anything. "It's okay, it was just a joke," he encouraged me. Then it was over. No one questioned my lack of a diaper as we combed the sandy campsite for trash. Technically, I was supposed to wear it until we got to the docks, but instead I was freed from the humiliation. I was able to enjoy my final hour on the lake with the hot sun bearing down and the wind in my long hair as the boat sped toward the docks.

That something which led Bunny to end my misery was a trait I would see demonstrated many times. It was at the very least sympathy that he had for his little brother. I was eleven and awkwardly near to tears in front of an unforgiving group of scouts who were all older than I was. He felt that and reached out to help me. But the trait was much deeper than sympathy. Bunny was not in general a soft sympathetic person. He was not the type to adopt animals, feed the homeless, and take Christmas gifts to the poor. At least, not individually. His heart did not bleed for individuals. His cause had its aim on a group much larger than a

Boy Scout troop. It was a movement against worldwide injustice. It was the whole community of the homeless and the poor and minorities that he had concern for. He had an innate sense of fairness, and so many things in the world seemed unfair. As if he knew the right duration of my Kangaroo sentence, and cut it off when the diaper was overdue. He seemed to know justice, not just in the rules of a boyhood game but a huge universal justice that extended to all humanity.

The fight against social injustice was one of the main factors leading Bunny away from our faith, and the seeds were sown at a young age. It didn't seem fair that men and women were treated differently in the church, or that few if any Blacks were part of the church, or that wealthy successful people made up most of the leadership. But these were questions you didn't ask in Sunday School, or if you did, you were ostracized as "intellectual" or questioning. Bunny had those questions. His faith never overcame his reason. If man could not answer the questions of inequality, and God was not available to answer them, then there was no sense in being loyal to a church. There was no reason to believe. There was reason to serve, and Bunny's charity was as great as or more than my own. But it was charity and service for mankind, for universal justice, for the intellectual reason that service makes one a better person. Not because God requires it.

Bunny believed in congruency. If you did not believe in the church, then you should not attend. Mom still fights him on this—if he would just attend church, just for the sake of his children. But he cannot do it. He cannot, in good faith, attend and listen and pretend to have faith when in fact his mind does not. It would be incongruous to himself. Funny that Dad used that concept so often—that man should be congruent with himself. It was Dad's explanation of his own faith—that he indeed felt a spiritual connection, and despite his own intellectualism it would be incongruous with that spiritual feeling to ignore it and disbelieve the church. Despite what he saw as conflicts in the church, primarily in its leaders, Dad could in good faith disbelieve or ignore it. Bunny had the same belief, congruent and true to his inner feelings. But his core did not feel that spirituality, and the belief in congruity instead led him away from our faith.

Kangaroo Kourt was only a tiny blip of my Lake Powell experience. The place was a scout paradise, and remains my favorite place on earth to visit. It's dreadfully hot, forcing people into the 80-degree water at least hourly to try and cool off. There are no trees, no shade, and rare clouds. There are sandstone bluffs to climb and explore, find red-sand beaches, and enough water and space for hundreds of boaters to hardly see one-another.

Doc, though a dentist by trade, packed more sugar and treats for three days than we would enjoy in a full summer at home. We had to wonder if he was trying to acquire new patients by rotting our teeth. Hostess pies, Ding Dongs, licorice, Oreos, and pop. Each person was allowed two cans of soda pop per day. The proprietorship and guarding of the pop became an issue much larger than merit badge requirements. Some wanted to take all their pop on the first day and hide it in their tent. But the 110-degree daytime heat would readily explode the aluminum cans, and the sticky mess was a sleeping-bag nightmare. The pop had to be sheltered in Doc's thick canvas army tent, and then taken out a few six-packs at a time to chill in iced coolers each morning. Unfortunately the tent fortress was easily penetrable from behind, and five-packs were common. Also, whichever boy was allowed to choose the daily pop had a great deal of power. He was essentially deciding which flavor would run out first. Invariably by day three the grape and root beer were gone, and the sissy lemon-lime and generic cola that were left were only slightly better than fresh water.

We went to Lake Powell in a 1978 Ford LTD station wagon, a monstrous vehicle. The wagon had fold-up seats in back for a total capacity of ten passengers, assuming all the equipment was tied to the roof. Sport Utilities and Minivans were still a decade away. Bunny and his friends often took the back seats where they could play Scrabble for hours on end, munching Skittles as we drove through Southern Utah. The LTD had 350 horsepower, and towing a twenty-one-foot Fiberform Cuddy boat was easy, even with two canoes, heavy camping equipment, and cans of food (including several cases of pop). Our "scout-mobile" rivaled any Hummer of today, and was known for indestructibility. Doc had led some thirty-plus boys to Eagle Scout rank, through hundreds of summer camps, swimming tests, snow camps, and other excursions. Occasionally there were more boys going to camp and Doc would have to borrow his brother Bud's wagon: same light green color, same faux-wood paneling, same gas-guzzling raw power.

The annual June Boy Scout trip to Lake Powell was the highlight of my year. It came just a week after school let out, and was the perfect start to a hot summer. We began early in the morning and headed south six hours through the small towns of Nephi, Salina, and Hanksville. Sometimes we'd stop at Capitol Reef National Park and have sack lunches and a dip in the river. But no one wanted to delay long in getting to Bullfrog Marina. By noon it was 100 degrees and we were anxious to get the boats out into the water. It would take several more hours to transfer equipment from the car to the boats, and then shuttle the boys from the dock to our campsite. But finally after a long day of travel we arrived at the secluded spot. Now we were free to cool off in the water, set up tents, and have our first pop.

Troop 385 went to the same campsite each year, and depending on the water level we might have more or less sandy beachfront. It was a calm inlet where we had little interference as we worked on canoeing, rowing, and swimming. The two "diving rocks" were almost a quarter mile out, at the entrance to the bay. Bunny was on the swim team at the Salt Lake Swimming Club, and could easily swim the distance to those rocks. I was on the diving team, and not much of a swimmer. I knew I couldn't swim that far. The difference was not just which sport Mom had randomly placed us in, but represented a notable contrast between Bunny and me: his athleticism, muscular build, and raw power, and my agility, grace, and orderliness. Swimming was a sport of direct competition with others in a series of heats, while diving patiently awaited each individual effort. He splashed and kicked and moved water, while I flipped and bent and tried with pointed toes to make the smallest splash possible. I could not swim to those rocks, even on low water years. Instead, I paddled Doc's superfast yellow canoe out, and then showed off by doing back flips from fifteen feet up the red rocks.

"Mona" was another high jump, a cliff just around the bend which we named after a small town along the Interstate-15 drive. She ranged ten to fifty feet high from year to year, sometimes not worth paddling to and other years a frightening dare to plunge from her lofty height. "Mo-naa!" we would yell as gravity pulled as down.

Beef stew was our traditional first night meal. More often than not the stew wasn't ready until dark, and the gnats were invisible in bites of meat and potatoes. We were assigned in patrols to prepare the stew several days ahead. Depending on how much parental involvement there was, a scout might have delicious homemade stew with perfect beef chunks and tender potatoes, or he might be begging Doc to open a can of pork and beans instead. Food at Scout Camp was never short if you didn't mind canned vegetables, canned beans, stale bread, and tiny dry out-of-season oranges.

My first year at the lake I learned to water ski, and it quickly became my favorite sport. Years later I realized a helpful trick during the hundreds of dry college lectures I sat through. If ever I started dozing, I forced myself to daydream about waterskiing. Suddenly my heart was racing, and I felt the cool water splashing over me, and the tightness of a life jacket holding me in, and the sensation that friends on the boat were watching to see if I could jump the wake. It didn't exactly help me pay attention to the college lecture, but the daydream woke me up every time.

Waterskiing didn't come easily, though, and the patience exhibited by our Assistant Scoutmaster was remarkable. He drove the Fiberform into a tiny little bay where the water remained calm all afternoon. There Matt Stevens, a fifteen-year-old neighbor, helped me as I awkwardly put on the two small skis and tried to hold them upright while bobbing up and down in the open water. "Hit it," I'd say timidly. The boat pulled the rope handle right out of my grip. The boat circled, Matt helped me balance, I held on to the handle, and we did it over and over again. I had been snow skiing since seven, but holding the rope for waterskiing was more tricky. Finally I stood up on the water and held on for a hundred feet. That was enough. Some combination of confidence building and coordination training clicked into place, and I suddenly started a lifetime of waterskiing fun.

The second year I got up on one ski, "slalom" as they called it. Again the balancing act, some encouraging me to drop a ski while others touting the advantage of getting up on one. I chose the latter, and found one ski much easier in many ways.

When Bunny found out that I was slaloming he was livid, he having been unsuccessful and this his third trip to the lake. That same afternoon he was determined to outdo his little brother, and though painstakingly difficult for the boat driver Bunny also became a slalom skier. I don't think he ever forgave me for doing it first. I wonder now three decades later as he takes my family out on his Mobius $60,000 powerboat if we aren't still trying to outdo one another on water skis and wakeboards. I admit that he has won the competition, but only because he owns the boat and gets more experience.

Mornings at Lake Powell were spent canoeing and rowing. Doc set up a figure-8 course around the bay, and we learned the J-stroke, feathering, salvaging a swamped canoe, and how to swim while fully clothed. The assistant and chief rower was Barry Sharp, a twenty-something next-door neighbor who was unusually friendly. It was said that the only date Barry had ever been on was with my sister Diana. Barry was gay, or at least that was the rumor. In 1980, "gay" was very much undercover. I had never heard the term openly used, or seen it in newspaper headlines the way we would in the nineties. And I personally highly doubted Barry's homosexuality. After all, rumors spread by Brian Knowlton were hard to believe.

"Notice how he's always watching your crotch in the rowboat," Brian said. "I tell you, he's a fag."

I didn't understand how Barry could be a "fag," and in my pre-pubescent years, I really didn't know what it meant to be one. Nevertheless the rumors persisted, and my friends caught on. My eighth-grade yearbook was full of my friends' comments about my next-door neighbor: "don't let Barry get you," and "'thsay' hi to our rowing buddy!" Bunny read my yearbook, and to my surprise was very upset about it. Homosexuality was so taboo in our culture that I fully expected Bunny, as well as my parents, to have the same anti-Barry sentiment as my friends. But not so, and I learned a significant lesson that day. Bunny was, above all else, open-minded and tolerant. He may have seemed like the ultimate macho anti-gay person, but instead he was accepting, liberal, and broadminded. Bashing gays was unacceptable to him. Bunny believed in the motto etched above the door in Mr. Webster's American History class, attributed to Voltaire: "I may disapprove of what you say, but I will defend to the death your right to say it" I fully expected my brother would become a great defense attorney.

When the hot sun finally went behind the red cliffs at the lake, we cooked our dinner and then cooled off with one final swim. I learned to wash my hair while treading water in the dark. The on-shore latrine was poorly built and embarrassingly open, and some of us had started the disgusting habit of defecating in the water and then burying poop logs it in the shallow wet sand. I don't think this was part of the official Boy Scouts manual.

Our second Scout camp of the summer was in Montana. Doc didn't care much for the formal camps with hundreds of boys, green uniforms, and military-like procedures. Montana camp was on a friend's private secluded ranch, and intended to be a fishing trip. The Big Hole River was teeming with wild trout. The fish were only six to ten inches, but a scout could catch dozens of them in a day. Matt Stevens set the record at eighty-six fish in our four days on the ranch.

My friends didn't fish much. Bunny and his friends played games in the tent, read books, or went on long hikes and talked about girls. My friends, as a junior high teacher once said, were more "vandalistic and ugly." We were waiting outside the junior high for my mom to pick up the carpool one Tuesday. My mom was always the late one, which was a great source of embarrassment to me. Mike grabbed an "itchy bomb," a seed pod from a local tree. He crushed it and stuffed it down Craig's shirt, which elicited a heinous response and soon the bombs were flying everywhere. Mrs. Pratt, an elderly English teacher, came out yelling at them and coined this phrase which was never forgotten: "you boys are vandalistic and ugly!"

One of my friends was cruel to animals, and took advantage of the Montana wildlife. He caught a frog, pinned it to a stump, the chopped it in half with a huge machete knife. He took a live fish and put it in boiling water as we all sat bored around a midafternoon campfire. He somehow caught a field mouse and pinned its tail to a tree while we threw Chinese stars at it. I was not interested in torturing animals, but I did want to shoot them. BB and pellet guns were off limits for Doc, so we sneaked them in the long canvas bags with our tent poles. We shot birds, fish, chipmunks, and finally got to the point where we started shooting each other. Our favorite target was the "potgut," also known as the gopher or ground squirrel. If you hit it just right in the belly, it made an unbeatable loud thud. BB guns would rarely kill the animal, however, but would stun it, slow it down, or throw it into a seizure upon which we would pounce on the animal and either shoot it between the eyes or smash its skull with a rock. Dallin Poulsen and I, both planning a future in surgery, took our pocketknives and cut open a gopher to see what his insides looked like. We dissected the tiny heart, opened his stomach to see partially digested grass, and cut out his liver in a sort of quasi-Native ceremony.

    The comparison of Bunny's friends and my friends was always of sad interest to me. Somehow we get matched up with friends because of similar ages, neighborhood proximity, or Sunday school classes. But I was never entirely comfortable with my friends. Bunny's group was intellectual, while mine was mischievous. His were upstanding athletic achievers who were adored by parents and neighbors, while mine were rebellious and became a terror to the neighborhood. Stopping in smoky Montana gas stations, his friends played pinball or picked up the sports section of a newspaper. Mine peeked at porn magazines while Doc wasn't looking, and the illustrious phrase "pink pubes and big boobs" would forever become a sarcastic part of our vocabulary. I wanted to be part of his group, not just because they were older but because I felt unnaturally thrown in with the bad guys: the C-students, the low achievers, the rebels. At thirteen we made a pact that we would never drink or do drugs, yet I watched many of my buddies turn to alcohol by age eighteen. They became thieves—small things at first, like candy bars from Foothill Drug. Then as we got older, it was more and larger, a Sony Walkman, a bicycle, and even a car stereo. "Five finger discount," one joked with me, or "midnight auto," he explained as the place he got parts for his Jeep. I was no angel, and once in hungry desperation, I stole an Almond Joy from the Old Faithful Lodge. But that was about the extent of it for me, whereas my friends progressed in their crimes and became a disgrace to me. I tried to never mention them in front of my family. I wanted instead to be included with Bunny's friends.

    At fourteen he caught me with a lingerie catalogue. It wasn't really mine, and I tried to explain to him that Mike had forced me to take it home and hide it for him. Granted I had taken the opportunity to view it with Mike, but then I wanted to get rid of it. Instead he pressured me into hiding it at home because I had a more private basement bedroom. I hid it in my ski pants, and never guessed anyone would rummage through. But within only a couple of days Bunny had reason to be looking for something in that drawer.

"Dude, you can't be doing that," he said.

"It's not really mine," I pleaded, and then went on my lengthy explanation of how it ended up in my drawer. But it was too late. He was disappointed with me. I brought shame to the family, just like my low-level friends. I was one of them, and certainly not the high caliber he'd expected in a brother.

Bunny was and is a man of high integrity. My parents would be shocked to hear me say that since he turned against our religion many years ago. How can a man of high integrity stray from the family faith? He strayed because he didn't believe, and as a non-believer he could no longer pretend to be part of the church, even if it meant offending his family. He's a man of deep character who sticks to his convictions.

Bunny was always honest. I learned at a young age that if you didn't want Mom to yell at you, then you came up with a lie. I was well versed in lying. The dollar I stole from Chris's bedroom I claimed to have found on the golf course. My friends and I were "playing Rack-O at Mike's" instead of toilet-papering a girl's house. I was watching TV at Mike Zackrison's instead of peeping in his sister's window after her shower. But not Bunny. He never lied. I have no doubt that he too was involved as a teenager in a few incidents of peeping, toilet-papering, driving underage, and even stealing. But he didn't lie about it. He wasn't afraid to tell Mom what he'd been doing, and even brag about how fun it was. He would readily confront Mom, and to argue with her. She came to appreciate his disagreements, and secretly cherished a son who was strong enough to argue with her—"debate," it was called, a respected talent which some inherited from the Huish family line. I was timid, cowering, afraid to admit my misdeeds, and sometimes ashamedly discovered in my dishonesty.

Bunny was forthright. He couldn't be caught in a lie because he didn't tell lies. He had no fear of adults, perhaps because he saw himself from a young age as one of them. He was intellectually their equivalent. He stayed out late, until 3:00 AM, with a girl once, and the next day he simply accepted his punishment and went on. He told it just like it was: they were out late, watching a movie, making out, and he simply didn't want to come home. "Grounding" was our usual severe punishment—no friends over and no going anywhere but school for a week. Bunny accepted that and fulfilled it honestly, almost as if he'd calculated the transgression and what it would cost him. Years later I once came in at 3:00 AM, and it was because I didn't have a watch, and the clock in the car was broken, and we got lost coming down the canyon, and other excuses. I complained at being grounded from the car and grumbled about it all week. I probably sneaked out a time or two, unable to fulfill the punishment that I'd never accepted or agreed to. He and I were clearly different.

"Slob" is what I sometimes wanted his nickname to be. Nineteen months apart in age, we could not have been more different in our mannerisms and interests. He was messy, I was clean. If Mom made scones with powdered sugar on them, his was invariably going to end up on the carpet. Once a week, Mom made a big bowl of piping hot spaghetti with fresh meaty tomato sauce on it. Bunny slurped it, and nobody wanted to sit by him. His side of the bedroom was a mess, while mine was nice and tidy. I once used masking tape to make a line halfway down the room and keep his dirty pants and *Dynamite* magazines on his floor. The brown puddle stain on our closet carpet would forever remind us of his sloppiness. We were painting the wall and he wanted to read the instructions to see the estimated drying time. He tilted the can sideways to be able to read it, and out dumped half the brown paint. He was a "jock," and I was not. He was good at manly team sports like football and basketball, while I was only good at individual and less masculine sports such as golf and skiing. He played loud music: the Who, Creedence Clearwater Revival, and the Doors. I kept it down with James Taylor, John Denver, and Kenny Loggins.

Bunny and I spent hours and hours doing yard work together. On summer mornings, we would come up to the kitchen only to find a long list of jobs that Dad had set out for us before he left for work. Mom urged him to do it, trying to keep us from summer boredom which ultimately led to pestering her.

Some of the jobs were artificially created and didn't really need to be done, but she was set on occupying our July and August days with more than Atari football and dismantling the minibike. And of course there was a certain guilt in parents who raised "mall kids"—city boys who had bikes and money and didn't know the back end of a cow. We were just one generation removed from "the farm," a nebulous pastoral setting which filled church sermons and story books. Neither of my parents was actually raised on the farm, though their semi-rural roots put them a lot closer to hay barns and hard work than we would ever see. City parents, therefore, needed to create work for their boys. And work we would. It was often said that unlike other neighborhood waifs, I would someday be able to meet a college sweetheart and assure her of my childhood upbringing, "I knew how to work."

Sometimes my parents would pay us, and naturally Bunny as the elder would make $1.25 to my $1.00 hourly wage. Other times the jobs were simply expected as part of our family duties. Bunny would start with the necessary music arrangements while I was assigned to get the shovels and wheelbarrow. He wired an extension cord out to the distant parts of the half-acre yard and plugged in a small black "boombox" which was covered with flecks of paint and smudges of mud. He had cassette tapes of Jim Croce and Billy Joel, or would borrow Cat Stevens and Boston from Chris's collection. We took off our striped tank tops like real workman, wearing only cutoff worn-out Levi's with our "skivvies" boxer shorts hanging out. We dug up the myrtle to plant sod and extend the grassy yard, then the next year dug up the sod to plant myrtle so that there was less grass to take care of. We weeded, planted, dug holes, trimmed bushes, then weeded some more.

I was a slow and meticulous painter, and Dad decided to pay me per job rather than per hour when assigned to paint the swing set bright green or the lounge chairs red. Bunny was a quick and sloppy painter and would have two chairs done to my one, but with splotches of redwood stain on the artificial turf of the back patio. We painted the black rod-iron banisters, the white rain gutters, the cedar fence, and the cream-colored patio table. We fixed railroad ties, shored up leaning tree branches, and turned soil in the garden. We mowed lawns together, both our lawn and several neighborhood lawns that Dave had procured in the years before. As I got older, I was assigned the more detailed and slower tasks of trimming and edging, while Bunny plowed through thick grass with our self-push Snapper mower.

I saved my money, and he resented a little brother who had more money in First Security Bank. He spent his on LP records, movies, and going out with friends for shakes. I was miserly and would only occasionally buy Tootsie Rolls or Starburst for myself, and certainly never for anyone else. Once my mom bribed us into dressing up as "Minute Men" for the church play in the 1976 bicentennial celebration. We each received two quart-sized glass bottles of Fanta grape soda, an unimaginable reward up to that point. Bunny's soda was gone within a day, but mine was slowly savored, one capful at a time, and lasted two weeks in the basement fridge.

Work took us to the Mikado Japanese restaurant. Just as city boys need a yard "farm" to learn to work, they also needed somewhere to occupy their Saturday nights. That left one night for friends, and one to work. One night for dating and girls, and the other weekend night taken entirely by restaurant work. So starting with my oldest brother, each of us spent one night in seven working at the Mikado. I started at the tender age of twelve when Jeff Bennion, a friend of Bunny's, was sick and unable to make his shift that night. Somehow Bunny convinced my parents that I was ready for the work which three brothers had done before me, and next I knew I was dressed in blue slacks and old leather "boat shoes" and on the Route 29 bus downtown.

The Mikado is where a boy became a man. Not just from hard work, which I had done in the yard for many years. But in life experience. It was the world, set apart from the shelter of home, church, and neighborhood like Manhattan stands apart from Mayberry. Located in the heart of downtown Salt Lake City, the Mikado was a bustling family-owned restaurant that attracted Salt Palace convention attendees, Marriott Hotel dignitaries, NBA basketball players, and travelers and tourists from all over the world. It was all the things I'd heard about on the news: diverse racial groups, homeless people, gangs, Second South hookers, druggies, and the rich and famous. But it was right there in front of me, tangible and malodorous, every Saturday night.

Bunny and I went in at 4:25 PM to begin vacuuming (why do you need to vacuum before and after a shift?), setting tables, loading ice buckets, handwashing fine tea sets, and eating as much teriyaki chicken as possible to prepare for seven hours without food. Unlimited soft drinks, which we consumed heartily, but no break for food until midnight. I was never officially "hired" but simply tagged along with my brother, who told the manager that I was filling in. That was the start of a ten-year career at the Mikado, rising from busboy and dishwasher to the job of sushi waiter and finally the highly prestigious position in my later teens as host (maître d').

Dressed in our short colorful Japanese coats, we watched as the mass of metropolitan humanity came and left. They laughed, partied, talked loud, and ate, all behind thin rice-paper sliding doors. We knew every repeated song on the Japanese music tapes which played overhead. Native waitresses, fully dressed in kimonos and heavy makeup, flurried about and yelled in thick accent "bus-a-boy" whenever we were needed. Patrons sat on the floor in traditional Japanese style, making cleanup a difficult and active job. We reached under tables for stray jumbo shrimp, occasionally nibbling on the remains if it seemed intact. The mats had to be brushed off, the wine glasses carefully cleared, and the greasy tempura tables wiped down several times. Naturally the manager took a liking to me because of my meticulous work, sweeping up each crumb and carefully wiping down tables. But Bunny was the workhorse. He carried huge tubs filled with dishes, then came back for more. I did the job well but slow, while he got the big jobs done and had the muscles for more.

Every New Years Eve of my young life was spent at the Mikado. We would host some five-hundred dinner guests between 6:00 PM and 1:00 AM. While my friends got together and celebrated the New Year, Bunny and I worked hard and nonstop clearing and setting tables. When finally the last of the drinkers had partied enough, we relaxed. Non-alcoholic wine was brought out for us. The music changed to the radio. Curried chicken and rice was served, and sometimes leftover steak or sushi. The employees danced in the bar, ignoring the fact that we all smelled of cigarette smoke, sweat, and sukiyaki sauce. Once the boss's daughter, and year my senior, asked me to dance. I was fifteen by then, and shared three awkward minutes of slow dancing with a stuck-up girl whom I otherwise detested. But it was New Years

Eve, and she was drinking real wine, and my exhausted body and mind seemed a little more attracted to her slender figure.

Bunny was eighteen when he stole a bottle of daiquiri mix from our workplace. It was the worst thing I'd ever see him do. My man of integrity, my big brother, my pillar of honesty. He and his friends enjoyed homemade frozen concoctions (sans alcohol) on their game nights, and it was much cheaper to swipe from the restaurant storage than to buy at Dan's Grocery. But I didn't think Bunny would do it. I was shocked by it, and worse yet when the boss caught him. Mark, the owner's son, counted a piña colada bottle missing from inventory. He simply walked up the stairs from the bar, unzipped Bunny's backpack which was hanging on the coatrack, and pulled out the bottle. All of this right in front of me, and without saying more than "I found it" to himself. I thought Bunny would be fired on the spot and have to call Dad for a difficult ride home. But nothing was ever said. Bunny continued working his shift through midnight, and never interrupted his weekly Saturday job. The manager knew he was a strong worker, and his value as an employee easily compensated for this foolish incident.

My value was less certain. I wonder if I had been caught if I could have survived, and how it may have affected my future in work and school. Bussing a table one busy night, I slipped the waitress' five dollars into my pocket. I finished clearing and setting the table in my usual way, but Sachiko caught up with me in the kitchen.

"Do you have my five dolla'?" she asked. Sachiko was American born, but put on an accent to match the other waitresses.

"What?" I replied innocently. I was unloading dishes, didn't look up at her. Bunny was next to me, and quickly surmised what had happened.

"There was a five-dollar bill on table twenty-three, and now it's gone," she said.

"I didn't see it," I replied.

"I know it was there. I saw it before the people left."

"I don't know," I said.

"A little mystery." Then she walked away in a huff. The rest of the night was uncomfortable as the story spread with other waitresses. They eyed me with suspicion. Bunny said nothing to me. It was one thing to steal a bottle of daiquiri from the restaurant, but quite another to steal from a woman. "A little mystery." The guilt in that phrase would remain with me forever.

Five dollars seemed like a lot at that age. It was more than an hour's wage, including tips. It meant that I could stop at Seven-Eleven after work and buy a doughnut and hot chocolate, knowing I wasn't spending any of my own hard-earned money. But that five dollars was the hardest earned of my life. I'll never forget the feeling of taking this money from someone. Not just a store, but a real person. Sachiko was married to a Caucasian ex-soldier with a bad back. She was the breadwinner for him and three kids. She worked five nights a week as a waitress, and ran a sewing business out of her home. Five dollars meant a lot more to her than to me, and I would never be able to forgive myself for taking it. I never confessed to Bunny that I'd taken it, but I'm certain he has suspected me of it all these years.

Years later I saw her from a distance. We were in Yellowstone National Park and I chanced to see her at a scenic overlook just off the road. I wanted to run up to her and confess, then hand her a twenty to compensate for what I had taken. I had planned it for years, that someday I would repay her—mail her the money, or send it through the restaurant manager. But I couldn't do it. She was with others and I was shy and couldn't even approach her. I argued with myself that the incident was so far back as to be forgotten. We drove away and I never saw her or heard about her life again. But the guilt remains with me.

Bunny and I had run for two hours. The beautiful forest gave way to switchbacks through low bushes with occasional rockfalls interrupting the trail. For the first time I started to feel the real fatigue of forty miles. I'd kept up my intake and energy pretty well, but this was much further than I'd ever gone before.

"I just need a little pit stop," I told him.

"No problem, man," he replied. "You feelin' okay still?"

"I'm fine, just maybe need a bathroom stop." I headed off the trail fifty feet to a small stand of scrub oak. I had no tissue or toilet paper, and I knew this might be clumsy, but I had to try and relieve myself of some rumblings in my lower abdomen. I pulled down my pants and squatted, but nothing happened. False alarm. I tried to relax, but squatting took more energy than standing upright. I put myself back together and walked slowly back to my brother.

"All right man, this is it," he said.

"It" was around the next bend. At the forty mile mark is a sudden steep snow-covered hill, a thousand feet vertical in less than one mile. Several climbers could be seen pacing up the steep slope against a backdrop of snow. I couldn't see anything at the top, but I knew there was an aid station up there. Station #9, just before the nine-mile descent all the way back to Vivian Park. This was the last uphill push.

The "hill of death" was the single most difficult thing I've ever done in my life. I started strong, each step almost a full stride up the mud and then snow. But then I slipped once, and breaking my fall pulled at already aching muscles. Each step was slick, and I found I had to kick my foot in sideways and make a step for myself. I tried following someone else's step marks to see if it was easier, then tried the untouched snow to see if I might sink in and get a better grip. Step after step, like climbing stairs, slipping down one for every few forward. Bunny was ten steps back, slowly and steadily climbing as if trying to push from behind. We had stopped talking. He could see how hard it was for me, and didn't know what more to say.

"The trail used to go around at this point," he finally broke in when we were three-quarters the way up. "John said they changed it because of a snow slide over there." He talked about the race organizer as if he knew him personally and was in close contact with him. "Almost there," he assured me.

I said nothing. I was so slow, and so physically drained. A few climbers passed me, but I hardly noticed. My steps were very small, edging my way up that mountain. In all of my training I had never felt this way. Hitting the "brick wall" was something I had experienced as I trained beyond fifteen miles. I had learned to tank up on carbohydrates and water, and to get past the lactate threshold. But this was like ten brick walls. The feeling of exhaustion was so complete, in every aspect: physically, emotionally, spiritually. The peak of that mountain felt like the nadir of my life. I had climbed to the depths of humility.

There was no turning back, and so I knew I had to get to the top. But the top was so far, and the hill so long. When I finally made it, I slumped to my knees. Then I fell forward and began sobbing.

"You made it dude," he said, glancing around him to see if other runners were watching us. I lay there in a heap, head down on my arms just above the rocky soil. I could not move. I could not believe anything could be so difficult. I briefly considered the tales I've heard of all the most physically demanding things in history: death marches, Everest, slavery, the atonement. I was whimpering, and I knew Bunny could hear me but I couldn't stop.

"That was so hard," I finally said softly. "I didn't think it would be so hard." I sat there for several minutes. Bunny stayed quiet but held a strong and reassuring stance. I was the cheerleader in high school, not him. He was self-strong and invincible, the one who can and will do anything. He encouraged and supported me by doing, by showing the way, not by pep talks.

I was finally able to get up, limping heavily. "Okay," I said with a laugh that comes after tears. "I guess we go on." He smiled barely, and gave me that look of confidence again.

"We're here, man—just down in those trees."

I walked gingerly down a slight hill and into a stand of pine. The whole area was covered with snow, and a guy with long hair and a gray beard was melting snow in a big pot over a fire. There was no water source at mile forty, and this guy had volunteered to llama pack in the equipment to melt snow, though I didn't see the llamas. A table was set up with the usual snacks, and I had watermelon and peanuts.

It was time to separate. Bunny had almost ten miles to go back, then drive out before dark. I had ten miles to descend and finish. He had come to support me, to "spot" me through the hardest part. He had seen me through the hill of death. He had seen me at the lowest point in my life, knowing that the memory of that challenge would be the highest point in my life. Bunny was always there. All of my childhood experiences. Childhood photos, family trips, work, bunkbeds. He is a part of every memory that I have. And it was no coincidence that he was there at that moment.

Separating was a familiar scenario to us. When he left for Yale and I was studying English at the university, I wrote a poem about our parting. The airport construction was maze-like, and he guided me through in the same way he was leading me in life. Leading me through childhood, now into adulthood, off to graduate school. It was awkward when I shared that poem with the family. Bunny was not a touchy-feely person. He was not a hugger. He and I did not express emotions well, if at all.

"All right kid," he said in his high nasal voice. Mom paid thousands of dollars to a speech therapist to help his voice develop. He needed a voice to match the intellectual stature and career goals he would achieve. But Dr. Fingerle's "ga ga" voice exercises didn't help much.

"Thanks, man," I said. "I wish you could finish with me."

"Yeah, I've thought about going out, and then you could drive me back, but I don't know what that road will be like in the dark." It was unusual for him to care about something unknown, rather than to face the challenge and danger. I think he wanted me to go at it alone from here out. I think he wanted to support me a little ways, and then let me finish alone in glory.

I forced a hug on him. Sweaty, muddy, chilled from snow. But I had to show him I meant it, well beyond the "dude" and the reserve of our usual conversation. I wanted to tell him how much I loved and appreciated him.

I didn't watch him go. He told me later how many runners joked that he was going the wrong way. He slid down the steep snow hill then ran the narrow trail back to his car, and would call me at home later that night. But now it was my time to finish this race. I turned and faced a partially melted avalanche below me, and the trail which tiptoed down through the snow weaving through the fallen trees.

Chapter 7: David, the Master Angler

Dave could do anything, or so it seemed. "Noodles," named for his lanky stature from birth, had reached successes that I would never reach. He was a multi-millionaire before age forty, a lawyer turned horse trainer who hit it big in a real estate deal that he partnered with a wealthy friend. He was the favorite uncle, fun to wrestle or to tease or to initiate water fights with the nieces and nephews while their own grumpy parents tried to keep order. Dave had a business persona and learned the art of human interaction many decades before I would figure it out. He was a public relations man, knowing the value of a firm handshake, a shared laugh, and a confident face. He ran for public office, sat on several important committees in the prestigious Park City area, was chosen for a prominent position in the church, owned a condo in Cozumel, slept in late when he wanted to, dressed very casually, and generally had achieved the successes that someone like me thought most important in life. It's hard to hide my jealousy, even underneath my admiration. Dave is five years my senior, and as the second oldest brother he was always the one I emulated and envied.

Ironically, Dave could never do what I was doing. He would never make it on that mountain. He was not a strong hiker, and had a bad case of altitude vertigo and motion sickness. He never made it up King's Peak, which is a story that will be told for generations in my family. I was only fourteen when Dad took three of his boys plus Dave's best friend to climb the highest mountain in Utah. We drove in through Wyoming to reach the distant trailhead, and started hiking late on a Friday afternoon. That was our first mistake, and a portent of things to come. As darkness fell we were out of the forest and into an open valley where we planned to camp at Henry's Fork Lake. But the valley was huge, and small trails led off in every direction. We each carried forty-pound packs, and had been hiking for four or five hours. Hungry for dinner and exhausted from the packs we spent over an hour criss-crossing the southwest part of the valley in search of the lake. Two hours after dark, we finally found the lake and set camp at the first open area that we came to.

My dad had climbed the peak before, but had recently received "shortcut" directions from a close friend. The next morning we started out according to those directions, hiking directly south to Cliff Lake and then scrambling up the steep rock slide to the ridgeline. We planned to be up and down by 3:00 PM to avoid the daily midafternoon thunderstorms. We each took a canteen of water and a small amount of trail mix and some beef jerky.

It was after noon before we reached the top of the rockfall and could look down at the crystal green Cliff Lake. From here the trail was unclear, but it appeared on the map that if we headed directly east toward King's Peak and tried to maintain our elevation around the ridge we would eventually get there. But that ridgeline went on for ever and ever. By the time we reached Anderson Pass and finally recognized clear trails coming from the north and south, it was after 5:00 PM. The afternoon storms came late, but rolled in with fury as we stood at the pass. Despite the wind and oncoming rain, Dad agreed to let us "rock hop" up this last part of the trail. The peak was just a half mile away, and we were excited to be so close at last. But there is no trail and no easy way up that half mile. Hopping between huge slick boulders we soon realized that even a small amount of rain was a detriment to our footing. Then the rain came stronger, and Dad called us back to the pass. For a moment I could tell that Dave and Bunny were going to defy him, but as visibility was lost and the wind pelted heavy rain on us, even rebellious teenagers had to concede it was time to get out. We would never reach the summit.

Running down from Anderson pass there was no shelter for several miles. We were exposed far above the tree line, soaked and cold as the storm beat on us from every direction. Dad and I were ahead when suddenly a bright flash of light surrounded us, and I simultaneously heard and felt a deafening crash of thunder. We turned around to see Dave and Jim some hundred yards back lying on the ground.

"Get down and stay down," Dad told me, pushing my body against the rocky ground and emphasizing I needed to lay right down on it. "Stay here."

I watched as he ran to them. He was almost fifty years

old, but a strong hiker and appeared unusually athletic as he quickly dashed back to check on the boys. Bunny was midway, and he pushed him to lie down on the ground as well. Dave was just getting up as Dad arrived. It was not a direct hit, but a very close lightning strike, which knocked him down and stunned him, or "buzzed" him as he described the feeling. The two of them now cautiously started toward me, guarded for another strike at any moment.

"You've got to stay low and walk fast," Dad said when we were all together again. The rain was loud as it hit his poncho, and he had to yell at us. "Don't stop until we get to the trees."

We descended in the opposite direction from the Cliff Lake "shortcut." While the real trail was several miles longer, it was clearly our best safety at this point. We held together tightly as a group and moved quickly down the mountainside.

It was dark when we reached the first trees. The rain had stopped and the sky suddenly became clear and bright with stars. Here we recognized why hikers want a shortcut to King's Peak. The established trail was an easy hike, but it was unbearably long. When the trail finally reached the treeline and turned west, we recognized on the map that we were only halfway back to camp. We were an entire valley east of our tents, and had another ridge to climb and then the Henry's Fork valley to cross. There was nothing to do but pray, which my dad offered with humble tears, and then began the long walk. Our food was gone, canteens empty, and all but Dad were regrettably unprepared for rain, darkness, and now the cold clear night.

By moonlight, we followed a wide and well-established trail. I led the pack, and had received the nickname "mountain goat" earlier in the day. Dave frequently stopped, begged just to sit for a moment, then lay right down in the dirt.

"We've got to keep going," Dad insisted as he pulled Dave's much taller body upright.

"I'll just sleep here," Dave resisted, over and over. It was the first time I became familiar with hallucinations. Dave was confused, his speech garbled, and he reached for things that were not there. I was anxiously fearful for his life, and for all of us. Dad could not forgive himself, and appeared both strong and insistent that we move on and also regretful and angry that he'd led his boys into this situation. Bunny and Jim helped walk beside

Dave as we navigated the ridge, reaching the top by midnight, then descended into Henry's Fork. It was the longest walk of my young life. We fell into bed at 2:00 AM and could hardly move the next morning. I could hear Dave's cries as he pleaded for Dad to bring him water and food.

It was the only time in my life that I felt superior to my older brother Dave. Perhaps that's why the memory is so vivid in my mind: the rocks, the trail, the moonlight, and Dave's hallucinations. I was the mountain goat hiker, while he was plagued with fatigue and dehydration and altitude sickness. I was strong and determined to hike King's Peak, returning two years later and successfully doing it. Dave moved on to fishing and horses and never cared much for backpacking again.

Little brothers are always just that: little brothers. I am certain that I treat Bowser Todd the same way, like he's still riding that Big Wheel and playing tag with his friend Russie. It's hard to treat each other as adults, equal in standing, with childhood long behind us. I can never catch up to Dave—I'll never be as old as he is, never as tall, never as accomplished. There was just this one time on King's Peak where I felt bigger. And perhaps now on Squaw Peak I was seeking that same feeling.

Dave was not a hiker. Then why did this phrase "Dave could do anything" come to me as I descended from Squaw Peak? Why did I imagine that Dave could successfully navigate these difficult few miles when I knew that he couldn't? He would never have made it as far as Hope Campground, not through the mud, not that many miles. He would have been sick. He would have turned back long ago. Of course Dave would never have even entered this race or had the crazy desire to run an ultramarathon. At least not without a horse. His life was centered around horses now. Twenty years after our King's Peak failure there was talk of doing it again, a "boys' trip" getaway and adventure. By then Chris and Todd had bad knees, Bunny and I had already successfully climbed the mountain once, and Dave said he would only do it on a horse. I don't like horses. And I don't like sharing the trail with people who climb mountains on horses. The boys' trip was a golf outing instead.

After the great hill and the aid station, the trail descends ten miles starting with a series of avalanches. The slick trail was dangerous. Not so much in that you'd fall off the mountain if you slipped, as there were trees to run into if you slid more than ten feet. But dangerous for injury. By now my body could hardly adjust to even the smallest slip. The muscles didn't catch and pull like they should, and each slick step was a painful reality that my sense of balance was lost. Falling a few times added to the muscle injury, and I allowed myself to just sit for a few seconds and anesthetize my legs with snow. Sitting there, I thought of lanky long legs skiing down the off-limits chutes on the back side of Solitude Mountain. I thought of all the adventures Dave had led me on.

Noodles was the unofficial but natural leader of a band of neighborhood boys. Sometimes I was part of that band, invited to climb the ladder up to Clint Bullock's attic hideout with the older boys. A dim bulb revealed bare rafters and fragments of shag carpet as the boys bragged about the great hideout they would make of this attic. It was a singular privilege to be taken in by my older brother in this way.

When the Route 29 bus was just a dime, and the freedom of summer vacation dragged into August boredom, Dave took us downtown. He was thirteen and I was eight, an unthinkable journey for kids in the current day of abductions and other dangers. But in the midseventies in Salt Lake City there was little fear of such. The most frightening obstacle was a dirty haggard old man who carried a cardboard sign and pushed all his belongings in a shopping cart and asked if you could spare some change.

Downtown adventures included the Deseret Gym, the ZCMI mall, Jeanie's Smoke Shop, and of course my dad's office. We proceeded in that order, off the bus just before it makes the turn by Temple Square so that we could walk up the short hill to the gym. The D.G. was an enormously complex series of dark hallways and empty stairwells. I'm not sure where those hallways led to, but I imagined racquetball courts and basketball gymnasiums in separate areas below that big roof. The pervasive smell of cotton candy and popcorn required strict discipline in avoiding the D.G. snack bar and saving our hard-earned allowance for ZCMI mall treats instead. Dave led us through the hallways, past the barbershop for old men, beyond the corridor where I faintly heard the calm music and wildly imagined women's leotard-clad bodies stretching out in yoga, and to the locker room. There behind a glass window a pear-shaped man with greasy red hair and a thin tank top handed out locker keys.

"Don't lose your key," he warned.

"We won't," Dave assured.

"Pin it to your suit," the man demonstrated. Then he pressed a loud buzzer, which allowed us to push through the door.

It is in this place, the D.G. locker room, that it is said my father received the remark about his hairy body that none of us will ever live down: "one more dip and you would have been a bear!" Repeated at every family swim gathering, that comment pretty well explains one of the embarrassing inheritances of the Allen boys. That being said, at age eight the only embarrassing thing in the locker room was my dissimilarity to the grown men around us. I sheepishly disrobed, quickly pulled up my favorite zebra swimsuit with the gold belt, then stuffed my clothes and shoes in the tiny square locker. Dave helped me negotiate insertion of a dime, followed by turning the key, then carefully pinning that key to the inside of my suit.

The Deseret Gym had two gigantic indoor pools, one primarily for swim and play and the other for diving. Here I learned to dive, and would follow in Dave's footsteps, joining the diving team at the Swim Club in the years to come. The one-meter board was bouncy, and he showed me how to crank the wheel and adjust the spring. While most kids casually walked to the edge and then jumped off in "cannon ball" position, Dave showed me poised stride of a real diver. Three strides, then the preparatory bounce, then a real dive. Despite that huge downtown place on a summer day, it felt like we were alone and the diving boards were never crowded.

The "high dive" was the ultimate feat at my age. Even climbing the ladder caused a bit of queasiness. I carefully held the rails as I edged out toward the end of the board. I felt like I was standing on top of that immense building, a feeling both exhilarating and terrifying. Dave taught me to squeeze a few drops of water and throw it off. Watching the drips on the water helped you gauge how far you were going to fall, and made it seem a little closer. He taught me first to sit on the end and edge forward at first, just falling to the water from a height not much greater than the "low board." Then I learned to stand and step off, holding my nose and closing my eyes tightly as I waited to hit the water. My big brother confidently stood atop that high dive and when it seemed that all eyes in the whole gym intently watched and waited for his perfect form, he delivered a 10-point dive, a one-and-a-half somersault with only a tiny little splash in the pool. I imagined applause all around, just like Greg Louganis at the Montreal Olympics.

With wet hair and wrinkled fingers we left the gym and walked past Utah's tallest building on our way to ZCMI. The Zions Co-Operative Mercantile Institution was thought to be one of the oldest department stores in America. We knew it as "the mall," and with little money to actually shop for anything, we were amazed mostly by its size. Indeed, walking around the mall was only thing we did. I wouldn't call it "window shopping," because our only interest in shopping was down the street at Wolfe's Sporting Goods. It was just walking, taking escalators up and down, marveling at the number of stores that were all under one roof. When the Crossroads Mall opened up across the street, no one could believe that a second gigantic mall could thrive there. What a big city we were becoming.

Orange Julius was my treat of choice. Saltwater taffy looked fancy as it stretched on a machine in the window, and See's fudge was what Mom would have ordered, but it was Julius for me. Dave negotiated the money, asked if I wanted fresh banana added to mine, and chose the size that would fit my budget. Then I sat overlooking the fountain and savored that tasty treat.

I'm uncomfortable to confess about Jeanie's Smoke Shop. It was on our way to Dad's office, that is if you took the back way around the block. We were not smokers, and could hardly stand the cigar smell that permeated the air as far as the bus bench in front of the shop. But Jeanie's attracted us for two reasons: bubble-gum cigars, and the off-limits magazines section at the back of the store. Kids were not allowed in that section, and Dave would never pretend to be going to Jeanie's for that reason. But purchasing our bubble gum one could just catch a scintillating glimpse of the titles *Playboy* and *Penthouse* and the big-haired blonde on the front cover. To very nearly participate in this double sin, pornography and tobacco, was like being initiated into a private gang of older men. When the bus and the pool and the mall would course through my mind in memory as I fell asleep that night, standing out most prominently would be the pink cigar and pungent tobacco and that possible hint of a paper woman almost seeable almost reachable just a few feet away from me.

Dad worked in the fancy wood-paneled offices of the First Security Bank tower. It was so different from our home that we hardly dared enter the place. Dave cautiously signed in at the guard's desk, fearing that one wrong move and he might pull his gun on us and accuse us of bank robbery. After all, we'd just come from Jeanie's and probably stilled smelled of vice. We took the world's fastest elevators to the fourteenth floor, just for fun, then came down again to the fourth floor. Our dress and adolescence were out of place in the elegantly carpeted hallways lined with thousands of leather-bound law references. Walking the back hallways we were apprehensive that at any moment Mr. Quinney, or Mr. Eccles, or some other bigwig mister would come after us and send us away. We strode quickly to the secretary's desk. Linda was a large full-faced woman whom I've heard that my mom had chosen as Dad's secretary, and she smiled and welcomed us with patronizing formality.

"David, Bryan, Richard, we've been expecting you, I'll see if Mr. Allen is in his office," she said as she picked up the phone. Then, "Mr. Allen, your handsome boys have arrived."

Dad must have sighed and braced himself for the boys to come in. He loved us and welcomed us, but the fragile art and furniture in his ornate office was suddenly at risk of being destroyed. We were fascinated by our dad's office, so different than the man we saw at home. Here he seemed to have power and authority. He was an attorney, or "lawyer" as I told my friends while rolling my eyes as I'd seen others do when speaking of politicians and lawyers. While not truly understanding what it meant to "represent clients" and to "draw up contracts," I knew that at any moment my dad could call Linda in and she would take notes and type up an important letter for him. I'd seen her do it. He received fruit baskets and fancy nuts from "business partners" at Christmas. We once enjoyed a weekend retreat at some unknown person's cabin as a perk from "the firm." In later years would come ski passes, the most treasured of all benefits, as Dad represented a ski resort. But at this moment, the best perk of all was that not too many turns down those austere hallways was a kitchen room with free soda pop, crackers, and tiny cans of apple and pineapple juice. It was, after a few brief moments in the office, to this location that we were treated. Having just finished an Orange Julius, a drink of pop or juice wouldn't seem so wonderful. But the tiny size of the juice cans and the ability to serve ourselves pop "on tap" was a great novelty. And at the office in that special little kitchen these things were free, the greatest novelty of all.

A Sprite and pineapple juice later, the office experience was over. Dad walked us to the front desk (probably helping us avoid mean Mr. Eccles), and under Dave's leadership we headed down to Main Street to catch the 29 bus.

After the steep snow fields was a long muddy trail. It was a straight trail that descended the mountain without switchbacks or changes. *Like falling off a mountain,* I thought. I pictured running down this trail with the ease and appreciation of one who has been climbing all day. I wanted to just run. Just run to the finish. It was easy now. Just run all the way out.

But I couldn't run. I was done running. I tried to run downhill, but my quadriceps muscles would not do it. My knees hurt with each step. My feet were in severe pain. I tried to run, but gave in after a few strides. *Just run down this mountain.* It seemed so easy.

Every twenty minutes or so, a runner would pass me. They looked at me in surprise that I was walking instead of running downhill.

"Almost there," each of them said. It was the typical runners' encouragement, even though we were still more than five miles out.

"You okay?" a hiker asked. She was on her way up the trail, enjoying a lovely summer evening hike.

"I'm good," I replied, hoping she wouldn't stop and try to help me in some way.

"Almost there," she said as she hiked on.

But I was not good. I was hurting. This was King's Peak again. Worse than King's Peak, this was purposeful privation. My body was starving—not my belly, but my whole body suffering from pain and starvation. I pulled out my emergency stash of sunflower seeds and raisins and tried to munch. I could feel my face pulled into a deep grimace, and I was unable to pretend a smile even when I tried. Step by slow step I was going to finish this race eventually, but two hours slower than intended.

    Dave could do it because he could make anything work out. He had an uncanny ability to make things work, even when others couldn't. He taught me things because he knew things. He was capable. He was competent. He was the Master Angler.

    Fishing is a sport that I've learned to hate. I hate it because I cannot catch fish. My eight-year-old learned to tag along with Uncle Bunny if she wanted to actually catch fish in the early morning at Trial Lake. The kids talk about the "huge" fish they each caught at Dave's ranch, and photos of them holding up a trout almost their own size adorn my office shelf. It was a pond stocked with desperate fish from the hatchery. In a stocked pond where the fish would bite anything we could catch fish, but otherwise angling was not my forte.

    Elizabeth is compassionate with me. Are you sure you want to try it again this year? I feel her ask. I'm on my way to buy new lures and a new reel to replace the one I broke last year. "I'm sure it's just being in the right place at the right time," she says, indicating Bunny's luck at Trial Lake rather than my lack of skill.

    "I'm sure I can catch fish this year," I reply with false confidence. But the tradition continues. I don't catch fish.

    Dave and I once fly-fished in Canada. It was an unusual spur-of-the-moment trip in late August when Bunny was in football camp and the older kids were in college. Dave and I, Coke and Todd, and my parents for a week in Alberta, Canada. Little did I know how significant this area would become in my future life, that I would marry a girl from Cardston, and we would live there for several years. But when I was fourteen Canada only meant one thing: fishing. Dave assured me it was the best in the world. I imagined catching as many cutthroat trout as Matt Stevens caught at Montana scout camp. We talked about it all the way up, barely noticing the wide prairies and small towns we passed through. We were in a rented motor home, an atypical expenditure for my parents. Inside the motor home Dave taught me how to hold the rod, ten o'clock to two o'clock, rhythmically throwing the rod with the elbow not the wrist. We cruised through Glacier National Park, a place where Dad nearly drove the big beast off the guardrail atop Going-to-the-Sun highway, and Mom screamed, "I see a bear!" which in reality was a big dog in the back of a pickup truck. Dave and I got out at a rest stop and practiced shadow casting. We must have been quite a sight throwing fly hooks into the weeds and then whipping them out again.

We arrived at Banff National Park in the stunning Canadian Rockies. "Lake Louise—one of the world's most famous lakes," Dad proudly said. Actually, there are no fish in Lake Louise, or at least if there were you wouldn't catch them through the creamy glacial water. We were disappointed that only canoes run at Lake Louise, no fishing. We tried to enjoy the scenery, but couldn't wait to get down on the Bow River.

"I've read all about the Bow River," Dave said. "It's one of those places that people dream all their lives of fishing. Like the Deschutes, and the Yellowstone—but better."

We finally fished the Bow River. I wore a huge pair of chest waders that Dad had purchased at a Canadian Tire store in Calgary. Dave loaned me an extra vest that he had, one with a thousand pockets to keep flies, line, wire cutters, and mosquito repellant. Mom let us take dinner in a hurry so that we could get out and fish. It seemed that everyone was determined to make me a successful angler. It was late evening and the fish were jumping everywhere in the calm eddies of that great river.

"We've got to see what they're biting," Dave said. He watched the air carefully, then swatted at a fly on his arm. He picked up the stunned insect by its white wings. "Mayfly," he said, "perfect."

Next we were changing our stonefly nymphs for mayflys. I could see why the vest came in handy as we would continue changing flies every few minutes. This was no worm fishing experience. When I was a kid, my dad would hook on a slimy worm and a red salmon egg and let us sit for hours. But this was "real man's fishing," actively changing with the environment and pursuing those fish.

"I fish because I love the environs where fish are found, which are invariably beautiful ..." Dave could quote John Voelker's famous testament by heart. And it was beautiful, the poem and the reality. Canada was all I dreamed it would be. In this serene and awesome setting, I felt a special attachment to Dave that we would cherish all our lives. More than anyone in the world I wanted to be like Dave. I listened to his music. I read his books. I copied his plaid shirts and old jeans.

In 1982, a teenager would be caught in nothing else but Levi's 501 jeans. At least in my area, where Wranglers were for rural cowboys and Calvin Kleins were for femmy rich boys who drove Saabs and wore RayBans. Levi's 501 jeans were the only cool thing for us, and Dave helped me with my first official pair. It was just out of elementary school, and before that time my mom had always helped me buy corduroy "cords" to wear. She and I shopped at Castleton's and ZCMI. But my dreams came true when Dave was assigned to drive me out to Mad Man Magee's to buy 501 jeans. He was just old enough to drive the 1972 Ford truck, and we headed south to areas of town I'd never seen before. In fact, he skipped Magee's. Magee's was known for clothes, but we did even better than that: we went to Allied. Allied was a real camping store with equipment, tents, sleeping bags, plaid shirts, and of course the rugged and true unwashed Levi's 501 jeans.

Buying unwashed jeans was a difficult art. You had to estimate how much the jeans would shrink on first washing, then subtract out the amount you thought they'd stretch after that. Dave told me one inch in the waist and two inches in the length was his experience, and so we carefully measured and tested a pair or two. They were gigantic on me, "swimming" in clothes too big as we'd say. One had to be very cautious not to "swim" with the end result, but even worse would be the dreaded "brownie" (too tight) or "floods" (too short).

We bought my first pair of jeans and took them home. But the experience was hardly over. "Now we've got to break them in," Dave said. New jeans weren't just to be washed and worn, but they must be worn out prior to wearing. He took my new jeans and threw them on the street as we stepped out of the truck. Literally threw them right down on the asphalt. Then he stomped on them, picked them up, and threw them down again. I caught on, but somewhat shocked at seemingly destroying new clothing. I threw them down on the dry grass and tramped over them. We stretched them between us, and then threw them against the brick wall. Some people, I later observed, even took scissors to the hems of new jeans in order to create that stringy worn-out look. As Dave and I initiated my new jeans, Mom watched it all from the front window and never interfered with our bonding experience.

Now on the beautiful Bow River we connected again. Dave caught a fish. It was a small one, maybe seven inches, but a feisty Rainbow. I watched him bring it in and de-hook it, then he released it back into the water. "White Caddis," he whispered loudly to me. I assumed he meant the name of the fly, but I had no idea what a Caddis was. He was upstream twenty yards from me, and motioned for me to come up. "Carefully," he said, motioning for my big boot waders to walk softly through the water so as not to destroy the stillness.

We changed my fly to a Caddis, then casted out in different directions. He spoke as he worked. "Watch those little eddies—see that little pool over there, just under the bush?"

"Yeah," I said, "but I just can't get it there." In this he was the Master Angler, able to cast his line in just the perfect direction and land it the perfect distance away. The dry fly floated on the water for a few seconds, and then he picked it off again.

"Just a few seconds on," he said, then waving his line back and forth in the air, "you've got to let them see it, but not for long."

It was hard for me to believe that a fish in the water could see and watch a tiny fly waving around several feet above the water. But that's why I'm not a great angler—I can't see what the fish sees, and feel the motions of the surrounding environs. I don't have the faith that fishing is really an art rather than just a mechanism. Dave had the uncanny knack of knowing where the fish were, and what they were thinking. It was not so different from his ability as a conversationalist with people. He could talk with people. He could ask about them, and show interest in them, and ultimately tell a lot about himself in such a way that made him seem similar to that person, whatever their station in life might be. I was naturally shy. In my many years as a physician I have learned to talk with people, and sometimes hear much more than I care to. But I only talk as needed—to extract data that might help in medical treatment. I talk with people as part of my job, not part of my interest. If I do come across some interesting fact that I share with a patient, such as an interest in golf or hiking, I usually have about two more sentences to acknowledge our common ground. Then I move on, either too busy to elucidate further, or too disinterested and shy to build a relationship. From an early age, Dave could take that moment and embellish it. A few minutes and they'd be buddies, whether a poor red-neck rancher or a polished political VIP. Dave could talk with anyone. He built resources. Not disingenuously, but with a good-hearted real ability to make connections with people and then use those connections and return reciprocal friendship. It's a unique skill, really. Some of us grow and develop relationships over time, while others of us recoil and shrink our lives over time. It's a talent I was not blessed with, or have been reticent to develop.

    His Caddis landed again on the water, floated one second, then it was gone, apparently sunk under water. For a split second I thought there was a problem, that the floating fly had sunk under the water and that wasn't supposed to happen. Then suddenly Dave's wrist pulled back and the glowing line went taught and exactly at that calm spot where the fly had disappeared was a splash and commotion and a fish came up flipping and jumping out of the water. It was amazing. It was fantastic to watch. A man twenty feet away had tricked a fish into biting a fake fly with a tiny hook on it, and now held that fighting fish tightly with a thin line of strong string. I listened as the silence was interrupted by the two different buzzing sounds of a reel as he wound it in, then let it out a few feet, then wound it in again. It was miraculous. It was incredible to behold. It was art.

    "Got him," he said, as he pulled the rod with one hand and reeled with the other. "There're lots of fish here, but you just gotta know where they hide."

    I said nothing at the moment. I wanted so badly to repeat that vision—to be the man standing twenty feet away from a fighting fish that I held tight on my line. But I had little faith that I could be that man. I would never be as tall, as confident, as mature as Dave. I took my Caddis upstream a few yards hoping to cast into new areas. Darkness was coming on fast now, and I was losing hope of feeling even a nibble, just a nibble to let me know that I could do that: I could trick those fish, and yank that hook, and pull them in. I tried a few casts in the eddies as he showed me. But I snagged into the bushes behind me. Dave was still close enough to watch me, and gave a look of sympathy at my snag. My big brother stood unsure whether to come and help me, or to stay with his passion and demonstrate how it's done right.

I do not catch fish. Fishing still seems intuitively a matter of luck rather than skill. But my disbelief is only from my personal experience. I vividly recall that vision of Dave standing in the Bow River, in the fading light, holding taut a long glowing line with a flipping fish on the other end. And it is hard to disbelieve. There is a certain dexterity in the sport. But I just can't achieve it, and so I don't believe. Year to year I try, but I just don't believe. And therefore, I don't catch fish.

The next day was more of the same. We fished Mosquito Creek in the high mountains. Mom decided it was too cold, and with her arthritis suffering, my dad drove her down to Calgary to fly home. I suspect there were other quarrels mixed in to her leaving, but it was not my place to get involved. When they both came back from Calgary, unable to catch a flight, we welcomed Mom with a simple, "What's for dinner?"

I did catch a couple of small fish after all those hours on the river, a couple of very small Rainbows. But I had certainly lost my enthusiasm. I wanted to catch big fish, and lots of them. I wanted to see a "hole" in the river, knowing that "Arthur," the famed big one from *On Golden Pond*, was deep down in that hole, and that I was the one that could lead him to the surface with a tiny feathered hook, which I made to look like an edible bug. Instead my lures coincidentally ran in to a couple of baby rainbow trout. Tiny, and few. I was disillusioned with fishing and with Canada. There was no magic in it for me. The rest of the trip was cold rain with very little fishing to do. I enjoyed splitting logs and playing cards instead.

The outdoors, and strength, and freedom were for me all melded together in my brother Dave. A "city boy" by birth, I grew up with the notion that life's highest achievement was not the polished wood desk in a high rise with my name etched in gold on the door, but instead the big black sky above the trees lit up by a roaring campfire and my sitting serenely beside it. "I love the environs where trout are found … and hate the environs where crowds of people are found, which are invariably ugly; because of all the television commercials, cocktail parties, and assorted social posturing I thus escape."

In the ten years that followed, my decisions would be heavily weighed by my ability to escape to the outdoors, Every holiday and free weekend had to be at least partially filled with a trip to Solitude, the Tetons, Yellowstone, Lake Powell, Sundial Peak, or at the very least a stroll up Millcreek Canyon. During a college summer in Cambridge, England, my greatest memory would not be Big Ben, or The Tube, or *Cats*, but getting caught in a beautiful rainstorm while riding an old bike through the farms of Grantchester. From day one of medical school I was determined to go into rural family medicine. It shaped my thinking in every way. I could not get enough of the mountains.

Dave took me to most of those places. Or he had been there before, like Cambridge where he had also studied, and met his wife. He spent a summer guiding float trips down the Snake River below the Tetons. When I visited him during law school he rented a car and took us far out of Manhattan and up to the Green Mountains of Vermont. We spent a cool night in borrowed blankets under a lean-to, near a wide river where I was grateful to lack fly rods. I think of that trip every time I see my daughter wearing the Green Mountains T-shirt he bought for me.

Dave and Jim and I often camped together. Driving through Kamas on our way to the Uintah Mountains, they had a well-known ritual for entering the national forest.

"This air is horrible!" Jim coughed and sputtered.

"Can hardly breathe down here," Dave joined in.

"And the noise here in the city—unbearable!" Jim said. Kamas is in fact a tiny town.

We drove by the sign. Welcome to Wasatch-Cache National Forest. Suddenly they rolled the windows down, breathing in deeply as the wind poured in our little VW Rabbit.

"Aah! Smell that fresh air!" Jim said.

"The wildflowers," Dave responded. As if everything had suddenly changed when we crossed that magic sign. I played along from the back seat, glad to be tagging along for another great adventure.

Dave is a great singer and sang with the high school Madrigal group. But he cannot remember lyrics. Crosby, Still, and Nash blared from the stereo.

"Teach, your children well ..." they both sang along.

"And so ... just a good-bye." Dave caught the first and last of every phrase, while Jim had every word memorized and could also tell a little history behind every song.

James Taylor was next. "Something in the way she moves ..." Jim and I once argued about the lyrics of that song. He was right. He sang it with more feeling than the original, and I knew he meant it for someone special. He pictured her as he sang along, closing his eyes and envisioning her smile and post-adolescent form. His voice was both beautiful and resolute, and I longed to have that serenading power. Little did I know that the love of his desire would be my younger sister in the years to come, and the parental disruption of that clandestine relationship would knock Jim from our lives forever.

Dave also sang along, losing the lyrics after the first line until the chorus, "I feel fine anytime she's around me now ..." My adolescent notion of girls, dating, and relationships were formed on those camping trips with Dave and Jim. At least from a boy's point of view. Starting at a much younger age I had experienced the girl's side in Diana: blissful one day and tearful the next, black roses on the doorstep, broken dates and broken hearts. I tagged along with Dad once as we staked out Mike Bailey's house to be sure he and Diana were indeed studying in the upstairs kitchen rather than making out in the basement. I remember going to a dance, or a "stomp" as they were called, to find Diana and bring her home for curfew. It was hardly acceptable and popular to be found and taken from a stomp by your dad and little brother. I came to know well the handsome, the funny, the laid back, the truck driver. We went skiing with Clark, fishing with Chris, and I even dressed up in an elf's costume to ask Christian to a dance.

Now I came to see relationships from the eyes of young men, and the difference between Dave and Jim. For Jim it was all about a sexy body. Granted in my culture actual sexual contact was prohibited, and "first base" (passionate kissing) was about as far as an eighteen-year-old had experienced. Still, it was the focus of thought and conversation. What did she look like? What was her shape? Was she fat, curvy, slim, sexy, and, most of all, big in the chest?

"If it is a breast it's really small," Dave said of the chicken piece he had just picked out of the Dutch oven roaster on the campfire.

"Biggest breast you'll ever get your hands on," Jim replied with a laugh. Here was Dave's chance to join in the fun and make a vulgar comment in return. There were no parents around, and no girls, and it was just the boys on a camping trip where anything goes. Dave was witty, at least as much so as Jim, and surely a return joke came to his mind instantly. But he said nothing. He took the chicken and covered the pot, moving on as if he'd not heard Jim.

I pretended also to not hear or understand the breast comment. But I recognized instantly that Dave was ignoring it for my sake. He was always cognizant of his example to me. He was a man, not a boy, mature at an early age and acting as an adult, a second father to me. Fathers talk of women and girls in respectful tones, with love and consideration. Dave was in to girls as much as Jim, but his attitude, or at least the presentation of it to his younger brother, was all different.

Liz Martin was her name. They studied anatomy together, another obvious fodder for Jim's jokes: "so, you never have to open the book, then?" But instead from Dave I heard about the creative way he asked her to Homecoming, and what her parents were like, and what she wanted to do in college. For all that my parents had taught me, it was Dave's example I best learned from and wanted to follow. While I'm certain that "first base" was a normal part of this teenage relationship, I never heard an inappropriate hint of it. Liz and Dave moved on from each other, but twenty-five years later I took care of her father in the hospital and he commented on what a fine young man my brother was.

"There is a place in North Ontario ..." Neil Young's unique voice took us to the place of refuge. We were minimalist campers. We never had a generator, or anything that required power. Music was for the car ride up, and ended abruptly when the car shut off. We avoided campground at all cost, and instead set up a blue Springbar canvas tent near the lake. We owned Pass Lake, or so it seemed. I became familiar with every trail, ever rock outcropping, the small island, and every possible fishing location on this high-mountain lake. It was two miles from the popular and crowded Mirror Lake, and we considered every other amateur angler and loud camper to be an intruder on our lake. It was the place I grew up tossing worm hooks at albino trout. The beaver dam had stolen any and all of my triple teaser and super duper lures. The parking lot reminded us of a time my dad was a hero.

    The Pass Lake parking lot is a direct offshoot of the highway, connecting on two sides and with room for about a dozen cars to pull off. Once when I was very young I was fishing or throwing rocks or untangling fishing line when a bloody scream and loud crash echoed through the trees and up to Bald Mountain. Someone racing up the highway had tried to shortcut through the parking lot, and at sixty miles per hour he'd slammed into another car. The sight of a fresh crash was unforgettable: shattered glass everywhere, twisted metal cars, and streams of blood on the pavement mixed with pine needles and small rocks. The sheriff would not be up for a half hour, and an ambulance almost a full hour away. Without hesitation, Dad offered to help the bleeding victim, dragging him to safety and bandaging his wounds. He rushed into our Amerigo camper, almost new at the time, and quickly converted the table into a bed. Then, to Mom's horror, he brought the bloodied man inside the camper to lay down and tend to his wounds. Never was my dad as cool and incredible as at that moment, and when the sheriff arrived to take over I thought he might deputize him right there.

    Pass Lake was our lake. It was the first place I would go to camp and fish when I had a drivers license and the VW Rabbit was mine. It was the place I would introduce Elizabeth to, trying my best to reassure her that bears did not exist in the shadow of Bald Mountain. It was my solitary retreat when, exhausted by studying for the Medical College Admission Test (MCAT) and just three days away from marriage, I found myself without a fishing pole, without so much as a jacket, sitting at Pass Lake in deep meditation for several hours.

    Camping at Pass Lake with Dave was both a step into adulthood and a reminder of childhood. It's been said that my dad never really fished there. Instead, he went from pole to pole changing line, re-hooking, adding salmon eggs, shaping cheese bait, untangling line, recovering a snag, and otherwise helping Diana, Chris, Dave, Bunny, myself, Coke, and Bowser. Mom stayed in the camper and might have caught a nap if it weren't for constant requests for a drink, a snack, a change of clothes, or her least favorite phrase to hear, "I'm bored." In the evening I cannot forget the feeling of a large overtired family coming one by one into the camper to settle in and retire. The commotion rises, and then calms. The close quarters annoys us, and then comforts us. My mother poured what she called a "puddle" into the small sink, boiling water from the stove mixed with cold lake water and soft sudsy soap. She would take from her hair a polka dot bandana, dip it in the puddle, then gently wipe from my face, neck, hands, and feet all of the collection of that day. Mountain soil, sunscreen, smoke, sticky pine sap, marshmallow, fish guts, cantaloupe, mosquito spray, chocolate, ash, and dirt. All gently washed with a warm sudsy bandana by my weary and worn-out mother before she steers me into a sleeping bag and I sleep the sleep of childhood.

  The camper was a must-have for a large camping family. My dad shared the same rough-outdoors attitude that Dave and Jim would later teach me, but when it came to adding a woman to the mix, and then babies, tent camping was no longer acceptable. The blue tent passed on to boys' trips and small groups, and the camper became the family vacation vehicle. It was an extra large camper, specially designed to sleep nine in various fold-outs and modifications, which affectionately became known as "the cave," the bunk, the snap-'n-nap, and the top. At number five, my place was forever of course the cave, a dark eighteen-inch opening below the fold-out bunk, with bedding formed with several bench cushions fitted together atop the lowered table. While confined and somewhat scary, it at least offered the benefits of bench height to fall from rather than bunk height, and offered relative seclusion from potential snorers in the group, and finally was closer to both the door and the potty than having to climb down from "the top." Of course the most coveted of all places was the comfortable double-mattressed snap-n-nap, which I was occasionally allowed an afternoon nap in but never a full night.

  Prior to having a camper, my father ingeniously built a small make-shift sleeping quarters on the back of the 1972 Ford "camper special" truck in order to drive to California and pick up the specially built Amerigo. It is my very earliest memory, not quite age four, looking back through the truck windows to see my brothers laying and sitting on porch-chair cushions and camping mattresses in the windy back of a pickup truck as we drove through the night to California. A few years later, that same truck and camper would take us on a three-week journey across the country, through Washington, DC, parked aside Central Park in New York City, then to Niagara Falls, Mount Rushmore, and in all an incredible adventure. Many trips to Yellowstone National Park, the Tetons, Disneyland, and San Francisco where Dad drove so close to the edge of the Golden Gate Bridge that an open window on the top of the camper was torn off. But of all the family vacations and adventures, Pass Lake was still our own.

Perhaps I've never caught fish like I did at Pass Lake, or at least have a memory of catching and eating fresh trout there. Dave probably caught them and gave them to me. In his late teens, Dave tried to compensate for our Canadian failure by taking me fishing on the Provo River. It was Fall and he was in college, but on a late Thursday afternoon we found the time to drive up to the Provo where it comes out of Deer Creek Reservoir. This was familiar territory for him, less than an hour from home and filled with great fishing memories.

"I've caught most of the fish here," he told me, "and thrown them back—so I know they're still there."

"Sounds good," I responded. I still had neither gained enthusiasm nor confidence for angling. We drove the truck down a steep and deep-rutted dirt road where no cars had been for a while. His secret location. His best fishing hole. He was sharing a confidence with me that was previously only known to our friend Jim.

We geared up in chest waders, vests, and the obligatory fishing hats. Dave had special polarized sunglasses that filtered the sunlight reflecting off the water. Maybe they were X-ray fish glasses. I just had my "glacier glasses," which someone at the Mikado had sold me, insisting they were name-brand Vuarnet. They weren't.

The holes were deep but the September river slow moving. Dave went downstream and gave me the advantage of going upstream. That way he wouldn't walk through and disturb the water I was about to fish in. I approached the river quietly, looking closely for just the right place to stand so that I could throw my line into just the right little hole. *I fish because I love the environs where fish are found.* I did love the outdoors. The dry hot smell of sage from the direction where the sun lit up the mountainside, and the cool wet smell of the river from the other direction. I loved mountains because they were strong and powerful, or my ability to climb them was strong and powerful. I have been swimming in a high mountain lake before, exhilarated by the frigid hard water in contrast to the tepid chlorinated backyard pools. I've skied through a raging blizzard, invigorated by the ability and desire to survive hard things. I've canoed through peaceful rivers, surrounded by deafening sounds of whippoorwills, crickets, frogs, waterfalls, and the repetitive dipping of my paddle.

    I eyed my standing spot, just across the river. From there I could cast into several deep pools in the eddies below the hanging willows on the other side. I started carefully down into the water quietly stepping through so as to barely disturb the sandy bottom. The bank dropped off and I went from midshin to midthigh in one step, feeling the cold water press the rubber waders to my legs. Then another step, this one again getting deeper than I expected. Then I continued moving forward, pulled and pushed by the force of the slow-moving water so that I couldn't stop. I quickly put my foot in front, the swung the other foot around, but falling deeper with each step, now to my waist, then to my belly. Recognizing I was going down into the hole too fast I abandoned any attempt to be quiet and started paddling backward with both hands, drowning the dry reel and pole that I held. I swooshed my hips back and forth, trying to regain some backward motion. But it was too late. The front lip of the waders dipped below the waterline and immediately filled with water. I could still stand, but the sudden weight of several gallons of water inside my waders dragged me down even further. Then I was entirely in, up to my neck and yelling for help.

    Dave didn't come immediately, and couldn't see what I had done. I held tightly to the rod in one hand, and pulled off the wader suspender straps with the other. I felt like a four-hundred-pound swimmer as I lunged back toward the shore while being pulled downstream. With each step up the waders peeled down and gallons of water spilled out. Finally, I fell on the sandy beach and drained entirely.

    Dave was coming up now. There was a slight smirk on his face at seeing an incredible picture of clumsiness, now beached on the shore. What a great photo it would have made.

But also on his face was that same look of sympathy, regretting that he didn't stay right by my side, and that I was again going to catch no fish.

"A little deeper than you expected?" he asked.

"I'm sorry," I replied. "I'm so sorry." And then I cried. It was not the response of a rugged man or an experienced angler who mistakenly dipped his waders in, but a shamed little brother who could not for all his brother's efforts catch trout with anything but worms and glowing cheeseball "power bait." My sense of failure was never stronger, and I felt that I would never be like Dave.

He helped me dry off and hang the waders and then we fished from shore for a couple of hours. I don't recall if we caught fish or not, but it didn't matter. I was done fly fishing forever. In twenty-six years I have not picked up another fly rod, even when the opportunity was nearly forced upon me.

For me, the only way to accomplish anything is the slow steady forward movement. Whether it be earning money, or schoolwork, or building something. There is no magic way to make it happen quickly. There is no sudden flash, no instant reward without the toiling hours of labor. I have admittedly tried a couple of methods for quick success. I've toyed with the stock market. I have written and published short stories, hoping for that sudden book deal that hits the bestseller list. But nothing works for me except the day-to-day regular work with a set schedule and a steady paycheck.

Of course I know of other stories. One of my closest friends became an instant millionaire when a silly table-top game he'd invented went big. He'd never finished college, which I have been afraid would prove to his kids and mine that college degrees are unnecessary. He was thirty, had a great family, and suddenly had lots of money. He joined the ranks of young rich businessmen who get their kids off to school, enjoy lots of leisure time, travel a bit, and no longer fret about long-term savings. Ever considerate to me, I had to wonder if he wasn't shaking his head when I e-mailed him that I was going off to Harvard. Yes, another academic degree. Another year of school, this my "twenty-fourth grade" as it were. Midthirties and unsatisfied and relatively unsuccessful, I was pursuing the only avenue I knew:

achieving another degree and hoping that it would lead to something big. There was no sudden millionaire in my fortune. There was no suddenness at all. Just the slow steady pursuit of progress in life.

  Granted my brother Dave has worked hard all his life, including a difficult three years at Columbia Law School, and several long hours at a law firm to follow. But when his ranch dream took off, and he was able to leave the office behind, we all felt a sting that I'm not sure has ever been forgotten. It was just as I was beginning my residency training, the hardest and longest three years of my life. How ironic that Dave was just departing from that conventional breadwinning way, and instead clearing trails with snowmobiles, taking clients up on horseback, and preparing the development of a huge ranch in the Uintah Mountains. It was hard work, and risky, but when it took off I felt the pain and sadness of being left behind. Left to plod along in my slow academic way, secretly hoping that someday I too could fall into that fortune. Maybe I would finally have time to pursue golf as seriously as I've wanted. Maybe I'd climb the seven peaks. But it was not my destiny. Dave could make things happen. He could do anything. He was the Master Angler. But I could catch no fish.

  Five miles of falling downhill on knees that jolted in pain with every step. I had stumbled, walked, and trotted, but had run very little of the last fourth of the Squaw Peak race. At the bottom of the steep descent was a valley that had been visible for hours. A field of golden grass still alight in the fading sun. The grass was remarkably dry for June, with thistles and other weeds already strong. A notable contrast from moist wildflowers that filled me with hope on the other side of the mountain. The mud was dry and caked now after a long day.

  The final Aid Station was at forty-seven miles, seemingly unnecessary so near the finish line. I was so close now, and would without a doubt finish this terrible race. But it would be a slow finish, plodding along through the grass, a step at a time. I imagined a zip line, or a gondola, or a four-wheeler, or even a horse. I imagined something that I could ride from here to there in a hurry. But in this race, as in my life, it was not my lot to go quickly. It was instead one painful step after another.

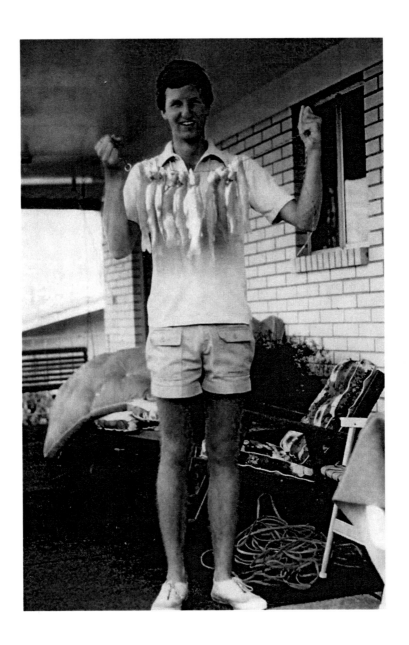

Chapter 8: Chris the Musician

When the phone rang, I knew it was Chris. Even without caller ID, and despite several calls since I'd been home, I suddenly knew and felt that Chris was calling me from Portland. It was the call I'd long been waiting for, and I felt my emotions well up as one of the kids answered the phone downstairs. For a moment, I thought about how silly it was, wishing on a phone call.

"Dad, it's for you," Madison said softly as she entered the room and brought me the portable phone. "It's Uncle Chris."

"Thanks, Mad," I said, and then paused and took a deep breath so as not to cry. Madison smiled then left the room.

"Fuzza! Howzit?" I greeted him in my usual manner. It's been almost thirty years since he wrote letters home from Hawaii with the familiar greeting "howzit?" Even longer since he acquired the well-known nickname "Fuzz," which described his adolescent curly head. But nicknames and familiar phrases don't seem to die in this family.

"Huna! The surgery man!" It was Chris at last, cheerful as ever. I'm not sure when or why he started calling me "Tuna," which then morphed into "Huna." It may have stemmed from the nickname "Junior," and during a time when Todd learned Spanish we started pronouncing things with a Chilean twist, like "dats a beeg burrito, man!" Hence "Junior" may have become "Hunior," and then "Huna." But I don't remember ever being called "Junior."

Huna was a late nickname, sometime in my thirties after Chris had moved to Oregon and I was in Canada. Maybe it was because we had moved, and as the family started to naturally separate geographically he felt a stronger need to bring us together emotionally. Holding on to extended family love meant nicknames, quotes from old movies we'd seen together, and funny phrases from family trips and experiences. We must have dozens of these, repeated most every time we meet and yet never growing tiresome.

Chris had the natural ability to bask in these childhood

memories, and yet move beyond them. He interacted with me as an adult, not as a little brother who's never grown up. My days of "Itchy" and "Chardo" were decades behind me, and Chris seemed to know that some childhood things were better left in childhood. We were once the Christmas card photo of kids lined up by age, height, and maturity. But now we are a circle of adults, with many decades of life and shared experience beyond our youth. Most of us are still guilty of calling each other by familiar names that should have passed when we became adults. Sometimes the names summon the relationships we held as children, like "Itchy" the picture of a short freckled squeaky-voiced kid. I suspect that Dr. Spencer Todd Allen doesn't really like to be called Bowser anymore, though he's willing to be loved and included by that name if it's the only option. Bunny is a grown man, and Coke a mature mother of five. Fuzz, Banana, Noodles. Chris wanted to preserve the affection that is in those names, but not the offense. He allowed me to refer to old times, and gave a courtesy chuckle to our reminiscence. Then he turned the conversation to what we are at present.

"Are you doing okay?" he asked. "Are you in pain?"

"No, I'm good," I replied, "pain has never really been a problem."

"Good, man, I hope they take good care of you." Chris suffered with a decade of severe chronic pain, starting in Hawaii with a hernia surgery. In addition to the usual litany of intolerable narcotic medications, he had turned to acupuncture, holistic medicine, meditation, and several pain and urology specialists to help. Chronic pain was one of the things that steered his psychological pursuits, and fostered the most empathetic person I know.

"No, pain's okay," I continued, "it's just hard to be cooped up and immobilized."

"Very hard, I understand." His goodness and understanding was so predictable that I knew what was coming next. I was suddenly embarrassed by it. I'd let myself fall for the same pattern: I complain, and he spins it into building me up. First he responds with sympathy, "I understand," the psychologist speaking. But then he comes up with a positive remark, not flattery and not over optimism, but a genuine truthful observation for which there is little to do but feel and appreciate his love.

"Very hard, I understand. You're strong, though. Your body's strong and your mind is strong and I can see you getting through this and emerging with even more energy. You'll think and you'll pray and you'll probably even write something profound and meaningful. Because you're like that—you've always been a strong-willed person, and powerful. Not 'power' in a negative way, over others, but strong positive energy to create things, and to face difficult challenges, like raising a family, you guys, you and Liz, you guys are incredible. You're going to be even better. How's Liz?"

I tried to soak in all he'd said, and to feel its genuineness. On the one hand, I always regretted my complaints. I knew as soon as I'd grumbled about being immobilized or being in pain or anything else that he would answer with a compliment so real and sincere that I would choke on my pessimism. At the same time, I relished his responses, momentarily basking in the light of brotherly love.

"Good, she's good," I replied, "I'm trying to be a good patient." I was tempted to tell him how hard it was going to be to have Elizabeth do all the housework, take out the garbage, and help get me dressed each morning. But I held back.

"You guys have got a good thing going, a good relationship and the big family thing, and all that. You'll do great, you two. You're a strong couple."

"Thanks, Fuzz."

"Hey I'm going to be in town in a couple of weeks and I thought maybe we could get out together with the brothers, maybe a little hike or something."

"Um, yeah, I ..."

"Oh you can't hike can you. How about a hot tub—can you hot tub? Let's tub it up at The Canyons together, that would be fun."

"Yeah, that'd be good—a pool, or a pond," I said, quoting our favorite line from *Caddy Shack*. "A pond would be good for you!"

He laughed briefly. "All right, maybe some sushi and a hot tub—boy's night out in Park City. Or steakhouse—I can do steak sometimes you know."

"Sushi's good," I said, "remember I used to work at a

sushi bar."

"That's right—the Mikado boy! That's you, you're a hard worker, you're a strong person with lots of energy."

"We'll see—I'm not feeling very strong right now."

"Hang in there, guys. My love to you guys, and the kids. Hang in there and you'll 'finesse this grommet' like you always do. You'll be back on top. Take care, bro."

"Thanks, Fuzz, thanks for calling." We hung up and I sat on the bed pondering for several minutes.

Long before any of his boys knew what "finesse" meant and what a "grommet" was, Dad used the phrase while threading a rope through a tarp hole as he was tying down tree limbs in the truck. We laughed at his big attorney vocabulary, and "finesse this grommet" became a favorite axiom applied to all sorts of difficult situations. Using the phrase, Chris brought together poignant childhood memories, love from my dad, shared brotherhood experiences, and the real encouragement that I could face challenges in my life. I pictured the Ford truck loaded with prickly pyracantha bushes on its way to the dump station. *Finesse this grommet*, I thought. I can make it through this.

The Squaw Peak 50 ended without fanfare. I ran the last several miles on a relatively flat and paved road with the occasional car driving past. Local picnickers packed up as coolness returned to the canyon and the sun was in its final hour. For fourteen hours I'd been out, exposed to the elements, running, hiking, and walking. Now nothing mattered anymore: what I ate or drank, what order I finished, or how badly my legs ached. It was all over now, the completion of a fantastically difficult day on the mountain. Now it was past tense, "done that," over and gone forever.

Elizabeth and my oldest daughter Heather met me a few hundred yards before the finish. They smiled and cheered and took pictures and video. Elizabeth seemed genuinely happy to see me, entirely without a trace of the anger we'd shared on the phone the night before. Most of all she was glad I was safe, but she was also happy for me. She knew how much this race meant to me, concealed through all those months of training but now present and open and she could join with me in the feeling of accomplishment. Later I would remember how much I loved her at that moment for her forgiveness and reciprocal love. But plodding down that road I felt numb to such emotions.

The finish line was poorly marked in the middle of Vivian Park, and a few dozen people sat around on the grass talking. Every ten minutes or so a runner would come in and a few of them would applaud and smile. I didn't see the tent and ran the wrong direction, embarrassingly turning around as someone laughed and yelled at me, "over here!' There was no "line" at the finish, or tape to break through. For me, number 151, there was a bit of applause, a token ribbon around my neck, and a quick pose with the race organizer. Then I stumbled over to a space on the lawn and willfully collapsed.

If I thought Elizabeth would disapprove of the long race, my parents were even worse. I'd not told them anything, not even that I was running in a "trail race" that Saturday. Elizabeth brought her cell phone over.

"It's your mom," she said, and then a grimace and raised eyebrows, which said "good luck talking with her."

"Hello?"

"Richard, we've been worried sick about you." It was the same phrase I'd heard for almost forty years, and always starting with my name—not a nickname. But this time there was unusual levity in her voice, not like I was in trouble but closer to a shared joke. I'd slipped this one past her, and unlike my twenties she was now much better at accepting the decisions, wise or not, of her adult children.

"Wow, you did it," she said. Wow was a word Mom never said with exclamation. It was as if she was quoting what the world would say, my same-age peers who would be legitimately impressed with running a fifty-mile race. But quoting with mocking tone, emphasizing that the only impressive part of running this race, or any such athletic feat, was in its stupidity. Nevertheless for my sake she tried to add a bit of oomph to her wow.

"You did it," she said again.

"How are your knees?" Dad was also on the line. "I'll bet your knees are hurting real bad.'

"My knees have been okay today," I said, "of course my whole body is exhausted, but the knees are okay." I didn't tell them that I had taken more pain pills that day then ever before in my life. I had regular doses of Advil and Lortab throughout the day, and even then the pain was hardly masked. But admitting that my knees hurt would be like confessing the foolishness of the whole endeavor. I had to at least act like it was a good decision.

"Well, I hope you can rest your knees for a time," Dad said. Knees were the Allen family focus. Chris had been through a couple of knee surgeries, Todd stepped in a gopher hole at fifteen and tore something that took him out of competitive sports forever, and Dad had arthroscopic surgery in his fifties. But the mother of all bad knee experiences was Grandma Allen. By age ninety, her knees were gigantic, painfully enlarged by severe osteoarthritis with knobby prominence greeting us from her wheelchair. Bad knees was the second Allen family curse, the first of course being bear-like body hair. Of course as a doctor, I was quick to point out that each of these individuals had entirely different knee problems, caused by different mechanisms, and afflicting at very different ages. But my knowledge of medical statistics did not, as it never does, account for the apparent blatant reality: Allen family bad knees.

"Yes, I'll take it easy, at least for a day or two."

"A day or two! Richard!" Mom replied. Part of generational gaps is the inability to be sarcastic together. Resuming running just a day or two after a fifty-mile race was so preposterous to me as to make for a funny joke. But my parents never seemed amused by exaggerations with potential serious consequences. To joke about "gambling away a paycheck," even if entirely without merit, implied that somewhere deep down there was a real thought of such foolish action. Even that implication was intolerable. Good decisions, especially financial, were a must. And I'd clearly already made the bad decision to train and participate in the race, so that further damage to your body was an intolerable thought.

"Just kidding," I said. "I'll take the summer off."

"Let Elizabeth get you home safely," Dad said. "And put some icepacks on your knees, doctor."

It was time to go. There was no one for me to talk to or socialize with, commensurate with the entire day except for the few hours with Bunny. I drank ginger ale and ate pretzels, wondering if I would ever want to eat pretzels again. We had separate cars, but Elizabeth followed me closely and called my cell phone with each little swerve or slowing just to be sure I was okay. Halfway home I pulled over, lightheaded and nauseated. I left the car in a McDonald's parking lot and went home with Elizabeth and Heather. Finally home, sixteen hours since I started, I dry heaved several times and felt faint as I pulled off muddy socks and a crusty dried shirt. Then I collapsed on the bed, without even the energy to shower, and I was out for twelve hours straight.

Three months later, I was in Dr. Scholl's office.
"Remember me?" I said. "We met at Squaw Peak—we sat by each other at the pasta dinner."
He did remember me and remembered that we'd talked about a little knee clicking that I was having. "Probably a plica," I'd said, and he agreed. Likely a very minor thing that would either go away, or perhaps need a cortisone injection. But nothing major. After all, I'd run a marathon in April, and then completed the ultra-marathon without any significant knee pain—at least not enough to limit me. But by the end of summer, I'd conceded that the ratcheting was not normal, and it was starting to be painful as I ramped up my fall training. Boston was my new goal—the king of all marathons. I would need to shave off a full minute per mile to qualify, what most would consider an insurmountable task. But Squaw Peak gave me the notion that I could do anything, anything at all.
What a shock, then, to discover that the curse of the Allen family knees extended to me, and that I was not invincible. Dr. Scholl was no less surprised to see an MRI showing a major cartilage defect in my right knee joint, a two-centimeter "hole" in the surface cushion of the knees. The running surface. Skiing, hiking, even golf—all of it was potentially out of my life now. Not yet forty, I suddenly and overwhelmingly felt the depressing reality of a major knee injury. I had just started teaching my girls to ski. We took Saturday hikes together, and I'd recently bought a new trail map. I'd turned my Squaw Peak spreadsheet into Boston calculations: the exact training that it would take for me to qualify for the 2010 Boston Marathon. Now I was told I would probably never be able to do any of that. My right knee was shot. I may as well have been diagnosed with a terminal illness.

Squaw Peak was difficult to recover from. Not physically, as a few days of rest and heavy-duty calories brought me back to normal. Within a week, I was jogging again, a couple of miles each morning just to keep loose. But mentally I could not let go of the fifty-miler. I thought about it with each pause in my daily routine. I went to bed at night, closed my eyes, and pictured myself along the course: the slick mud, the narrow lonely canyon, the snowy climb, the hill of death. The feeling was immense, filling my soul with an enormous sense of happiness and accomplishment. Night after night, my whole body was filled with a sensation of lightness, like I was flying above Squaw Peak and watching myself run. It was the greatest thing I'd ever done in life. Greater than the feeling I had when chosen as the graduation speaker at Harvard. Greater than my first big paycheck when finally a practicing physician. As great, and strangely similar in the emotions I felt, as the birth of my first child.

On September 26, 2008, I came down hard from Squaw Peak. The surgery went well, and Dr. Scholl was confident I wouldn't need the second surgery we'd talked about. But it was all tenuous, and very much dependent on my rehabilitation. For eight hours a day I had to sit or lay down with my knee in a "continuous passive motion" machine, slow cranking my knee joint open and shut. The fragile repaired cartilage could take no weight bearing, not even a smidge, for six weeks. I used crutches around the house, and a wheelchair working at the hospital. Just months after my colleagues and neighbors saw me training, running hard each day, now they saw the opposite. I was crippled, sedentary, extremely limited, and very discouraged.

That's when I thought of Chris. Wallowing in self-pity, I forced myself to recognize that Chris had given up skiing, backpacking, and running several years ago. He'd gone through at least two knee surgeries, but neither time did I feel any great sympathy for his limitations, his pain, and the lifetime athletic restrictions that he accepted so humbly. Now I felt his pain. I felt the suffering from so many patients that I'd so flippantly disregarded in the past, even as I tried to be a compassionate physician. Finally, it was my turn to wait in the waiting room reading old magazines, to see the medical bills piling up, and to feel the limitations of what I previously hoped was invincible good health.

Contrary to my self-centeredness, Chris's life was all about feeling for others. He was an expert in listening, understanding, and cautiously offering feedback without giving advice. The oldest son, he was the last of us to get a doctorate degree. He'd taken a different path in life. It was a path that met with my parents' disapproval: multiple relationships but still unmarried in his forties, wild hippie college friends without the same religious values, and too many years of schooling and work in the "soft" low-paying field of psychology. But in our adult years, Chris is the one we all secretly go to for counsel. Even Mom relies on his judgment and understanding. He drops what he's doing to talk at inconvenient times. He responds to e-mails with love and encouragement. He knows my kids and cares for them. We love Chris, and what's even better is the way that he loves us back.

Chris is a musician. In his charcoal drawing he is casually dressed with a saxophone in his hands, his afro of fuzzy black hair atop a warm smiling face. The sax was his main love, though it all started with clarinet in the elementary school orchestra. And from time to time, he'd borrow from the music shop and bring home curious different sizes of saxophones, once even a flute. For me, putting in the painful required half hour of piano practice was the daily drudgery of life. But for Chris, music was life. He would spend hours down in his basement bedroom, teaching himself the melody of a new jazz tune.

"Hey, little bro," he said, "check this out." I sat in the beanbag chair while he played along with Billy Joel's "I Love You Just the Way You Are." He played with feeling and emotion, as if serenading a beautiful girl instead of me. He closed his eyes and felt the music come through him, hitting every note as he practiced for an upcoming high school assembly. It was as if she were there, too. Lisa Myers, the seductive blonde who sang to him as he drove us to the ski resort on a snowy winter day. Bunny and I sat awkwardly quiet in the back of the Jeep Wagoneer as Lisa pretended not to notice little brothers and went right on with her song. Chris and Lisa didn't get much skiing in that day. Or he was playing to Stacie Wong, the fun-loving Japanese cutie who became a lifelong friend after the short teenage romance faltered. As he swayed and Billy Joel sang,

"Don't go changing, to try and please me," I could see them dancing together and laughing and staying out until all hours of the night. He played to Camille, the solid no-nonsense girl that he was engaged to for a short time. So many years I've seen Chris alone and wished things worked out with Camille.

Music was more than a teenager cranking it loud to escape his parents' voices. Music was mood and feeling. Chris did not put on a record for background noise. He played a song, a specific song, and then another to match or create the mood.

Seagull you fly across the horizon into the misty morning sun ... Nobody asks you where you are going, nobody knows where you're from. Chris absorbed the music, often alone with his eyes closed, feeling the meaning of every rhythm. Where most of us heard only lyrics, and Dave couldn't even remember that much, Chris heard tone, movement, and texture. Music was colorful, pregnant with feeling and emotion.

"Hey, little bro," he said, "check this out." I'd heard the introduction to Boston's "Don't You Cry" a thousand times, the hard-rock instrumental classic blasting through Chris's Klipschorn Heresy speakers. It was so powerful, even too much for me at age ten frightened that Mom would pound on the floor again and yell at him to turn it down. Music was his power and his trademark.

Music meant diversity. Dave settled on the folksy sounds of James Taylor and Crosby, Still, and Nash, and Bunny turned to harder sounds of the Who and Jethro Tull. But Chris maintained the full gamut of diversity, symbolic of his ready acceptance of color, religion, and personality. Earth, Wind, and Fire was as popular as Three Dog Night, Chicago, America, and Fresh Aire. He turned on Spyro Gyra to jazz him through his math homework, Bad Company to clear his head, Kansas while talking with a friend on the phone, and finally the Grand Canyon flute of Pierre Rampal to go to sleep. Music was funk and soul, style and art, feeling and expression. Chris introduced me to a wide range of heroes, from Kenny Loggins and Dan Fogelberg to George Benson and Lionel Richie, Harry Chapin Carpenter, and Cat Stevens.

As little kids we once set up a Tinkertoy concert, now treasured in its poorest quality on old eight millimeter home movies. I was the drummer with cymbals made of pie tins and a bass drum of a Lincoln Logs canister. Bunny played a guitar we'd made from cardboard. Coke danced and sang along. Flashlights hung from the ceiling with yarn, spinning round to create the effect of wild spotlights. We dressed up with bandanas around our heads and shirts wide open at the neck. Coke came up with a sequined dress from the dress-up chest of clothes.

"Jeremiah was a bullfrog..." Bunny lip-synced with Three Dog Night while I hit the drums, "was a good friend of mine!" Chris played his records for us on "the 1918," a 1950s turntable that we teased Dad about being much older. "I'm a rocketman!" Dad shined the bright camera light in our eyes while he filmed, the flashlights spinning around and the music as loud as that record player could handle. Mom laughed and clapped to see such fun, while at the same time disbelieving and dreading the pre-teen music influence Chris was having on our family.

Music was everything to Chris, and in an age before it was portable. He was in to music long before the Walkman and the boombox, and even when the Chevrolet Bel Air and other family cars had nothing but AM radio. Recordable cassette tapes became the rage, but compact discs and mp3 players were still a generation away. The lack of portability necessitated Chris and Dave's bedroom become home base for the ultimate groovy music hang out. When we moved in 1978, they found an unfinished basement the perfect opportunity to create that place.

The idea for redwood slats was found in a magazine. Diagonal slats on one wall, and on the other a most unique look: two-by-four redwood cut end-on to make small blocks, hundreds of them individually nailed to the wall in vertical lines. The other walls had a heavy grasscloth wallpaper. Bedspreads were black three-inch shag, and the desks and stereo cabinet handmade of dark wood. It was a place of texture for sure, an atmosphere of funky mood and rich character. Bunny and I tried to copy it as we grew into our teen years, but the look and feel could never entirely be imitated.

When Chris had saved enough money, half of the cost matched by Dad, he insisted on stereo components. I never quite understood the theory of component buying, and wondered why he couldn't just go to Sears and by the JVC stereo "set" they sold. No way. Each piece was carefully chosen by its specifications: the Kenwood 120-watt amplifier, Pioneer double cassette tape player/recorder, and Technics turntable. The crowning components were speakers we'd never heard of, but then never heard the end of: Klipsch Heresy. In that room was enough vibrating energy to break dishes three houses away. All components were carefully set into a custom-built wood shelf in their groovy room.

The ultimate test for this hi-fi sound system was an unheard of disco piece by The Salsoul Orchestra, an intense Latin rhythm version of Strauss's tune "Also sprach Zarathustra." This powerful theme won not one but two student body officer elections for me, both sixth grade and high school. It begins with a slow crescendo of helicopter wind and jungle monkey screams, building up with bongos and conga drums until the whole orchestra joins on a gong downbeat with the well-known tune made famous in *2001: A Space Odyssey*. The disco beat is irresistibly danceable for the five minutes to follow, laced with funky noises that sound like barking alligators, English hounds, and prop planes. Needless to say it was the bane of Mom's life to hear such noise rumbling from Klipschorns in the basement. But for me it was powerful music, inspiring in my short-lived pursuit of percussion, followed by the lifelong interest in jazz piano. I can still feel the colossal sensation I had while standing high above an audience of two thousand high school students. After the monkeys and threatening monsoon, the Salsoul gong peaked as I belted out a primeval yell and the spotlights found me, "SuperRich" coming to save the day. My contender, whose skit played up the mild-mannered John Boy Walton, didn't have a chance against the funky and powerful music Chris had recorded for me, with Dad's deep voice-over. "SuperRich!" I pulled off the unthinkable underdog victory for Student Body President. I owe the victory partly to Diana's posters, but also to Chris and that energy and that music and that incredible feeling that he had for life.

That exhilarating feeling, and the presidential leadership opportunity which followed, were so distant from me now as to make me weep with loss. I was an invalid, sitting helpless in my bed playing computer games while a machine held my knee and slowly moved it back and forth. As I thought about Chris and his music, I downloaded tunes from the Doobie Brothers, the

Eagles, and even found online the infamous Salsoul tune. But it disturbed me more than comforting me. It was an age of youth that has long since disappeared. Now in my fortieth year I was a responsible breadwinner and father, a remote distance from the little brother relaxing with free time on a shag beanbag chair and being inspired by Carole King. If standing atop that auditorium as SuperRich was the zenith of potency and power, I was now at the nadir, my most significant low in life. Not only immobilized as I recovered from knee surgery, but potentially never reaching another mountain peak again. I felt this physically and metaphorically.

    I would walk again, and I was grateful for that. Imagine a tragic car accident or climbing fall and the possibility of permanently losing a leg or having brain damage. At least I would walk again, and probably enjoy biking and small hikes with the kids. And there was golf. Golf was worth living for. If I could have my knee back for one purpose, it was golf. The thought of this suddenly filled me with a real desire to rehabilitate my knee. I sat up in bed and adjusted the machine, putting down the mindless computer game as if new focus on the knee would make it heal stronger and faster. There was always golf.

    I grew up on a golf course. I played golf officially at age seven, but used the Bonneville public course from age three or so. The thirteenth hole was my backyard, and became the familiar playground that most city boys can only dream about. In groves of scrub oak I set up G.I. Joe base camp, including a fancy zipline where my uniformed doll would swoop down and save Barbie. The golf course opened up my first job opportunity, selling cold Pop Shoppe on the fifth hole. Golf-ball hunting kept me busy for hours upon hours, and selling the best Titleists had me haggling with hobnobbers at the tender age of nine. As a teen I'd been chased by the "Jeep man" more than once on a late-night rendezvous. In winter I learned to ski on those hills. Like a Sherwood Forest, or a Treasure Island, the golf course was a land of endless possibilities of boyhood exploration.

    My dad was not a golfer, and Bunny and Dave only dabbled in it. They didn't have the golf gene that Chris and I shared. While I was hunting balls, Chris maneuvered free lessons from the head professional at Bonneville. He became friends with the golf shop junkies, the Luppinacci brothers and the Herricks.

In his green over-the-shoulder bag he carried the precious Ping Eye 2 irons, which he'd worked hard to buy used, and Nicklaus woods carefully protected with green fuzzy club covers. He spent hours of time mastering his short game, usually at sunset on the green behind our house.

Chris played high school golf and traveled with the team to seemingly distant courses, which I then dreamed about: Bountiful Ridge, Wasatch Mountain, and Willowcreek. I remember sitting in church and doodling golf course layouts on the back of the paper bulletin. I dreamed of becoming a professional golfer, uncertain how I would break the news to Dad who had me pegged for an architect.

As a freshman at Highland High, I found out about golf tryouts on the first day of school. That evening I was a nervous wreck, wanting with all my heart to make the golf team like Chris but knowing that I had nothing even close to his talent. Mom's attempts to encourage me were fruitless, and I considered abandoning the tryouts to avoid risking the terrible embarrassment I knew would be mine when my scorecard read 54 after nine holes. They were looking for near-par young golfers, not double-bogeys, I thought.

Chris found me in the dining room, hiding behind the curtains and staring out the window with moist eyes.

"Hey Tom," he said.

"Huh?"

"Come here," he motioned, "I want to show you something." I followed him downstairs to the favorite bedroom. Gladys Night and the Pips played on the stereo, "I can see clearly now the rain is gone …."

"How come I'm Tom?" I asked.

"Tom Watson," he replied, adjusting the music volume and looking through his records for one that better suited the mood. "I think you're like Tom Watson," he continued. "There's Nicklaus, and he gets all the attention and wins a lot. He's a great golfer, and he deserves it. But it's guys like Tom Watson who come along and quietly master the game."

"I can't even make the cut."

"You see, I don't think Tom worries about 'making the cut,'" he said. "He just goes out there and plays golf—solid, quiet golf like nobody's around."

"It's hard to pretend when I have to report a triple bogey on the first hole," I said.

"Yeah, but you've eagled that hole before—remember?"

"It was a lucky 5 wood that got me to the green," I countered.

"It was years of practice that came together for you. It doesn't happen every round, but you've got it in you. An eagle on the first hole—that's big, man." He changed records and put on George Benson, "I won't quit 'til I'm a star ... on Broadway."

"What if I screw up tomorrow?" I implored.

"Relax, just relax," he responded. "That's what you need—relax." He started to massage my shoulders. "I think if you just go out there and play like you play every day, and don't worry about playing with older guys that are seniors and have done this for years, just go out and do your best. Relax, and do your best. Have fun, man—it's golf, it's fun, it's relaxing. Be the ball, Benny."

I knew there was no way we could have a serious golf conversation without quoting *Caddy Shack* at some point, and I laughed with him and felt for a moment that I was relaxed. I was in the groovy bedroom, sitting on shag, listening to inspiring rhythms, taking counsel from my fuzzy-headed big brother who shared the golf gene. I realized that most of my anxiety was not whether I made the golf team, since chances of that as a freshman were slim anyway. But underlying was a fear that I would disappoint my older brother, and not be able to follow in his yard-long stride as I had hoped since first borrowing his "shag bag" practice balls at sunset on the thirteenth green behind the house. But now I felt and understood that disappointment in others was not a quality he held, and that no matter what happened, even if my Ping putter failed me, he and I would be okay. And would be okay forever.

I made the cut. Actually, I vaguely remember some slight discrepancy on the fifth hole where I reported a five instead of a six, as if not recalling the duff out of the trees, which nobody else noticed. But I can't imagine that I outright lied about my score. I just remember that there was some discrepancy in that round, and that when on the ninth hole we sat on the hillside behind the green and started calculating total scores, I was well aware that 46 was going to be the cutoff.

"Allen, did you shoot a 5 or a 6 on number five?" my scorekeeper asked. "I don't have anything recorded."

"I think I got a five," I said, knowing full well that a five meant I was in the top twelve kids, while a six on that hole put me at 47 and would likely ding me out. Jim Hatch, a fellow freshman whom I didn't know well at the time, shook his head with a sigh. He knew the scores too, and had already reported his 47. Three years later, when Jim and I served as student-body officers together, I felt that he never would forgive me for that "discrepancy." I don't know whether he saw what I had done, and frankly I don't even know that I had done anything. It's too far back in my memory. But I'll never forget that moment, reporting my 46, Jim sighing, and moments later the coach announced the Highland High Golf Team, of which I was a proud alternate member.

Mom was elated, knowing how much it meant to me. I'd spent the summer golfing every day on a fifty-dollar Junior Punchcard Pass at Bonneville. My white-soled Topsiders were grass stained, and my ugly Bermuda shorts that I'd cut from some thrift-store polyester pants were threadbare, especially the pockets where I'd stuff four or five golf balls so that I was ready to take extra "Mulligan" practice shots whenever I needed to (something totally unacceptable in gentlemen's golf). But more than anything I'd hoped for, more than the acceptance I felt during my first week in high school, more than hanging out with the big boys, seniors who gave me rides to Bountiful Ridge and Wasatch Mountain, more than anything I felt the great satisfaction that I'd achieved what Chris had led out on. Chris rarely golfed anymore, between knee surgeries, college demands, and traveling with the band. But deep down inside he still had the gene, and that was a gene and an experience which we shared.

Maybe we could golf together, he said. I lived in Canada, and he in Oregon. Or I was in medical school, too busy and too poor to golf. He set down the clubs for a lot of years. It was a difficult pastime to maintain, and neither of us ever really got out more than once or twice a summer. But there was always that possibility, maybe we could golf together. We'd golfed in Waterton National Park, watching for bears and deer as we hit through a spectacular mountain scene. We played in Oregon a couple of years ago, the Skamania Lodge "boys trip" with all of my brothers. We'd played through the red rocks of St. George, Utah. We've talked about golf dreams: Pebble Beach, Bandon Dunes, maybe even Scotland someday.

My goal of becoming a professional golfer ended by about age fifteen, not long after my freshman season ended. I didn't make the team the next year, and in fact I don't even remember trying out. It was no longer realistic for me, and I delved into academics and student government quite heavily. And I had watched Chris do the same, losing his passion for the game as the realities of college life hit. But there was always golf to dream about, and to bring us together. "Be the ball, Benny. Be the ball." Some families hunt together, or fish, or hike. We've done a little bit of all these things. We've backpacked to King's Peak. We've floated down the Snake River. Bunny and Dave now own a boat that we sometimes ski behind. But there was something special about golf. It's relaxing enough to talk and be together. We always walk and carry our bags, even thought we might afford carts on some courses. We enjoy the outdoors, the mountains, coastline, and rivers that outline the sculpted and man-made golf courses. It is just competitive enough to keep a little fun going, like wagering a milkshake on a birdie putt.

Most of all, golf was my childhood. I grew up on a golf course, and I have never entirely left the stands of trees, the green rolling hills, and the river winding its way through. To say that I knew Bonneville golf course is a gross understatement. I knew every piece of that land, as a golfer and as an explorer. I knew, and still know, every trail through every clump of scrub oak. More than once I stumbled through a cache of golf balls assembled in the same patch of tall grass by the golfers' dreaded slice off the second tee. I had trudged through that river many times, wearing my old holey tennis shoes and knee-high tube socks, dipping down in whirlpools where white balls collected off number nine after many a golfer risked carrying the green. I've escaped from the "Jeep man" late at night, the threat of his rumored salt gun enlivening my mind and body with great alarm, running through the break in the fence around the small reservoir and hiding behind the shed on the other side.

Chris used to lead us through Dead Man's Gulch, a small tree-lined gorge off the north side of the fourteenth hole. I will never know if any real man died there, but the rumors were rampant. A hanging, with a long rope strung from one of the high trees dangling above the cliffs. Or a shooting: two boys, brothers, shot while hiding in one of the small caves. A drowning maybe. All possibilities were vivid in my mind as we edged our way down the steep banks and into the river gorge. This was beyond where most golf balls were lost, and the purpose of our trip was adventure rather than hunting. Here we explored the forest, hoping to scare up snakes or gophers.

  The river ran through a four-foot-diameter conduit, and then fell off into a pool beyond the fifteenth tee box. The brave ran the fifty-foot pipeline, squeezing through the locked rebar on the far side and plunging into the pool below. The rest of us, the young and scared in that valley of death, climbed out and walked around, then toe touched only in that cold water. Chris was naturally supportive of toe-touchers, though he was old enough to lead the brave through the tunnel. Always inclusive and compassionate, Fuzz was not one to tease, pester, or make fun of his younger brothers. He seemed to feel what I was feeling, and had a depth of perception from his early teens.

  It's remarkable what little in actual conversation I can remember having with Chris. Dave and I would talk "man to man," he the father role, deepening his voice a bit and calling me Richard, and I the little brother eating it all up. Bunny and I were always talking, or more likely arguing. Sharing a bedroom for almost two decades, we were a part of each other's lives more often than not. But I don't remember talking to Chris very much. We were six years apart age, just enough that we never attended the same school. He was well into college or traveling or moved out by the time I was in my mid teens and had developed the ability to converse. And even then, I'm not really a conversationalist. I'm rather quiet, and I guess I could add boring to be with. Still, my reservation is probably not to blame for lack of conversation with Chris. It's just that Chris knew how you felt. You didn't have to say so much, but just listen to the music and he understood. He was not preachy, and rarely even now gives direct advice. But he listens, and seems to know. And he has a tune that will match or repair the feeling.

  Maybe we could golf together. The persistent thought of golf with Chris led me to a familiar childhood romp. It was three weeks after surgery on a beautiful crisp October Saturday when Elizabeth knew I had to get out. I was done with six hours per day of being strapped to the continuous motion machine, and I was cranky from being cooped up, and I would never stop being angry at the change—knee surgery—that had occurred in my life. As if to make things worse in my mind, I had to get out and see the mountains and breathe the air. We left the kids and went for a long drive. It was obvious where I was driving, even before I knew it. And Elizabeth didn't have to ask. She knew. It was a familiar place we'd not visited in fifteen years.

  The Cottage Farm is forty-two minutes from my home, in the beautiful Heber Valley. We passed the campground, the Wasatch Mountain golf course, and the hot springs, each of them escalating my emotions. Huge new home developments with fancy European names now cover what once was bare farmland. The valley has become a hot spot for cabin owners, a bedroom community to the overpriced Park City area just ten minutes north. A few years ago we looked at building a cabin in that beautiful valley, and even bought an acre of land near Deer Creek Reservoir. But it was overpriced, and I didn't really have the time or the know-how to supervise the construction of something, and I knew I'd never make that childhood dream come true. We sold the property within six months.

  I had not seen the farm in many years, having been away most of that time. It was sold after a couple of difficult years when the house was poorly cared for and some of the ten owners were not making their financial contributions. It was a sad but necessary step, according to my parents. Our family would move on to another era, perhaps buying a condominium in Jackson Hole or looking south to St. George. I had just graduated from high school when I helped my dad remove most of the furniture and put it in storage. A real estate sign was in front and would stay there for almost a year before someone bought the place. I had heard that a banker bought it and was planning to divide the land and build several homes, but I was never really certain of the story.

  Elizabeth and I pulled into the driveway on that October day and just stared for a moment. The gate with the "J.B." initials swung wide open, and the gravel driveway was covered with weeds. The huge trees that once surrounded the driveway were now stumps, having been infested some years earlier. The lawn was dry and brown. The pink paint was peeling badly. The famous silver roof had been replaced a few years prior with brown wooden shingles that were now cracking and had probably not been oiled since they were placed. That roof had cost a small fortune to replace, my father had told me.

I got out my crutches and we made our way around the grounds for a few minutes. The house was locked and empty. While I pointed out a few highlights to Elizabeth, we were both rather silent as we walked the gravel drive. The manager's house was boarded up, and no sign that anyone lived there anymore. A beautiful new house had been built just next door and not only eliminated the seclusion of the cottage but blocked the view of Memorial Hill as well. The barn doors were open and a couple of old bicycles still chained inside. We stopped in the corral and sat on the lava fence, again silent and somewhat mournful. Maybe I would be rich someday and buy the place back, I told her. Then again, it would never again be what it once was.

As the day drew on we got up to leave but made one final look through the barns. I ascended the old wooden steps to the hangman's room and before I had reached the wooden door the fond memories of my little sister and playmate overwhelmed me. I slowly squeaked open the door and there before me was that same room, only slightly more dirty. The white metal cupboards were there, just as we had left them. The gunny sack was unchanged, and the rope swayed in the rafters above as a breeze came in. And there on the wooden floor were the toys I had played with some thirty years earlier, probably left there by Bowser Todd just before the farm was sold. I stepped under the hanging sack for a moment and bent over to pick up a plastic toy. "This is my lion," I said to Elizabeth as tears filled my eyes. It was hard to believe that a toy would still be there, untouched these many years. I tried to go back and think of all that I'd been through in two decades: so much schooling, marriage, six kids, moving five times. Childhood was so far back that it was hard to recall, but now streaming into me like the light through the stovepipe hole with familiarity that was emotionally breathtaking.

"Time to take this lion home," I told my wife. With that she placed her arm around me as we descended the stairs and headed back to the car. We passed the dilapidated tennis court, the outbuildings where I'm certain some of our old bikes still rust away, the game room, the patio. We closed the doors and gates behind us. Walking on that gravel drive I felt that I could hear voices: Uncle Joe at the barbeque, Diana's girlfriends squealing in the game room, a guitar singer by the campfire, yelps of fun from catching fish and riding the minibike, castles in the sand box, acting out *Little House on the Prairie* in the barns, and Mom yelling out the back door as I hid in a nearby fort, "Richard Elliot? It's time to come home."

Lightning Source UK Ltd.
Milton Keynes UK
UKOW02f0801271216

290797UK00001B/293/P

9 781257 055142